The Next Wave

The Next Wave

The World of Surfing

edited by

Nick Carroll

Abbeville Press Publishers

New York London Paris

First Abbeville Press edition

Produced by
Weldon Russell Pty Ltd
4/52 Ourimbah Road
Mosman NSW 2088 Australia

A member of the Weldon International
Group of companies

Publisher: Elaine Russell
Managing editor: Dawn Titmus
Designer: Catherine Martin
Production: Jane Hazell

Library of Congress Cataloging-in-
Publication Data

The Next wave : the world of surfing /
edited by Nick Carroll.
    p.   cm.
  Includes index.
  ISBN 1-55859-162-1
  1. Surfing. 2. Surfers—Biography.
  I. Carroll, Nick.
GV840.S8N49 1991   90-20410
797.3'2—dc20   CIP

© Copyright Weldon Russell Pty Ltd 1991

A KEVIN WELDON PRODUCTION

JACKET PHOTO CREDITS
FRONT AND BACK: AARON CHANG
BACK: PAUL SARGEANT (TOP), JOHN CALLAHAN (CENTER
LEFT), JEFF DIVINE (CENTER RIGHT), PETER SIMONS (BOTTOM)
BACK FLAP: PETER SIMONS (TOP), DEAN WILMOT (BOTTOM)

Page 1: *Darrick Doerner, Sunset Beach.*

Page 3: *Martin Potter strolls a high wire.*

Right: *What right has Bronte Beach, Sydney, Australia, got to start imitating Hawaii? Good old Bronte, cringing beneath 15-foot (five-meter) swell lines.*

TONY NOLAN

Contents

Above: Modern surfing
is, above all, a spectacle — big
moves, color, drama and the
simple question: will he
make it?

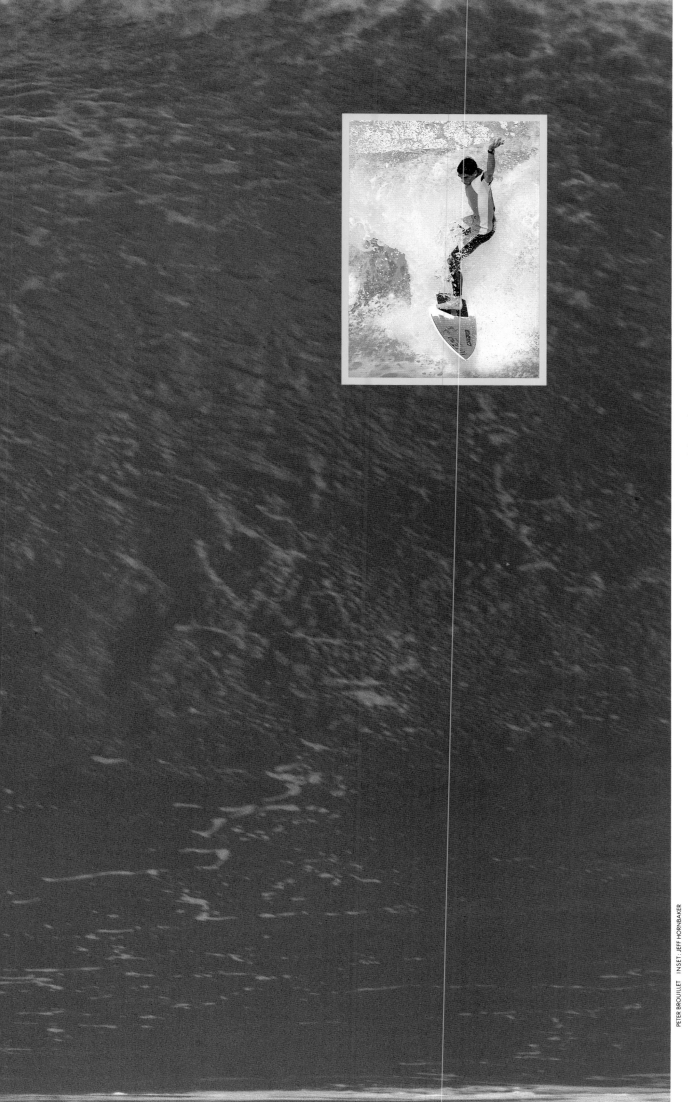

Giant Pipeline is where all your cool and experience pay off. Here Michael Ho takes a careful look at something almost too horrendous to contemplate.
Inset: *Cec Wilson.*

Introduction

"Why surf?" People all over the world have asked me that question. It seems as if no matter how often they ask it, they get no closer to an answer. Perhaps, like any human activity, the great sport of surfriding seems to tell us something about ourselves. What is the lure of the ocean? What is it that excites millions of people — kids, grandparents, mothers, business people and super-fit athletes the world over — to throw themselves into the salty sea, have huge waves crash down upon their heads and finally to ride a roaring swell into the sand so they can do it all over again? Why do they travel to all corners of the globe, always chasing the next wave?

Here is a book which answers these questions. For the first time it pulls together the talents of the best surf writers and the surf world's award-winning action photographers. Inside you'll find a fascinating essay on the great Hawaiian chieftain-surfers of centuries past; an accurate, witty tracking of the surf bug as it spread worldwide; a look at the crazy characters and the big-wave cult of the 1960s; a detailed analysis of pro surfing and its superstars.

And beyond that, you'll see spread before you in words and pictures the state of the art — surfriding as a mature, exciting sport. Come as close as you can without buying a plane ticket to the great surf zones of the planet: California, Australia, Indonesia, Europe, South America and, of course, Hawaii, where the biggest waves in the world spring up each winter to challenge the best surfers in the world. Visit the spectacular waves: Grajagan, Jeffreys Bay, the dreaded Banzai Pipeline. Meet ordinary surfers along with the heroes who've changed the sport. And as you do, see if the answer to the question: "Why surf?" isn't plain as the nose on your surfboard.

Nick Carroll
GENERAL EDITOR

*E*arly morning, when the sun suddenly jumps out from behind a wave and catches you at a critical moment, is one of the best times to go surfing. Here Cheyne Horan savors a moment at Bells Beach, Australia.

A Surfing History

This engraving of women
surfing, by the French artist E.
Riou, appeared in an 1873
travel anthology entitled Quatorze
Ans Aux Iles Sandwich
(Fourteen Years in the
Sandwich Islands).
Inset: Mickey Dora at Malibu.

Ancient Hawaii
THE BIRTHPLACE OF SURFING

LEONARD LUERAS

During the past thirty years, surfing – and surfers – have captured the attention of sports enthusiasts, fashion trendies and even intellectuals in numerous glamorous ways, but few people realize that this aquatic pastime has been enjoyed since perhaps the Middle Ages or earlier, and may indeed be one of the world's oldest and most "organized" athletic activities.

Since ancient times, centuries before high-tech waveriding craft were created, the people of Polynesia – and particularly the Hawaiians – have regularly been meeting at their favorite surfing beaches to compete in surf contests, during which avid spectators feasted, cheered and even placed property bets on their favorite surf stars.

Even the typical twentieth-century surfer's seemingly irrational dedication to and obsession with the sport is nothing new. Traditional Hawaiian chants tell about fine surfing days when Hawaiian waveriders would drop whatever they were doing – work, family, everything – to ride good waves.

When the surf was up, wrote the prominent nineteenth-century Hawaiian scholar Kepelino Keauokalani (1830–78), "All thought of work was at an end, only that of sport was left . . . All day there was nothing but surfing. Many went out surfing as early as four in the morning."

And if distant storms didn't generate suitable waves, anxious Hawaiian surfers would enlist the aid of a *kahuna*, a sorcerer, and literally pray for surf. The *kahuna* would chant loudly to the sea gods and lash beach vines "unitedly upon the

In the twelfth century Hawaiians recorded their feats of bravery with carved pictures, now called petroglyphs, in the lava rocks of the beaches. Occasionally the petroglyphs are exposed again by big swells, giving modern surfers something to think about.

16

water until the desired undulating waves were obtained," according to one chant. In some parts of Hawaii, the natives even built impressive stone *heiau* (temples) at which they would pray and leave offerings.

In the files of Hawaii's Bernice Pauahi Bishop Museum, the world's leading repository of things Polynesian, there is a 1919 archeological study written by John Francis Gray Stokes (1876–1960) that describes an ancient seaside *heiau* at Kahaluu Bay on the Kona coast of the Big Island of Hawaii which was identified by Kona Hawaiians as a "*heiau* for surfriders, where they could pray for good sport." Stokes doesn't write a great deal about this temple, known as Ku'emanu, except to say that within its confines was a bleachers-like terrace where spectators could sit and watch surfing and a brackish stone pool where surfers could bathe after a day's surfing.

In one Hawaiian chant that has been dated to about the twelfth century, the Hawaiians celebrate the surfing prowess of a great chieftain, and in yet another mythological "song" poetical stanzas tell about a serpent-sorceress who fell in love with a

handsome young man, and, in an attempt to keep him as her lover, gifted him with her tongue which she had transformed into a magical surfboard.

No early written accounts about surfing exist (because early Hawaiian traditions were passed down orally, in the form of memorized *meles*, or chants), but archeologists and art historians have discovered – on the islands of Lanai and Molokai – petroglyphs (pictures incised in stone) which depict early surfers on surfboards. These petroglyphic surfers may or may not predate the arrival of the whites (or *haole*) in Hawaii in the late eighteenth century.

Ancient surfing scenes (as recounted in collected chant sequences) were apparently fanciful, fun, bitchy, and sometimes violent. Woe betide the weaker of two surfers who became entangled in a love triangle involving a powerful woman chief, and even worse was the plight of an enthusiastic surfing commoner (of lower caste) who dared to ride waves that were *kapu*-ed (declared off-limits) by a surfing *alii* (high-caste native).

A collection of known Hawaiian surfing stories – together with similar Polynesian lore from

BISHOP MUSEUM

E. Howard, Jun. del.

I. Finden sculp.

Page 369.

S tunned Western seafarers took all sorts of different attitudes toward the Hawaiian surfers, but one thing they had to do was record the action. Left: An early surfing scene, engraved from a drawing by one E. Howard in 1831. Opposite: Not a great deal of good came from the European invasions. By the time this photo was taken, in 1890, hardly any surfers were left at Waikiki.

FRANK DAVEY, BISHOP MUSEUM

Samoa, Tahiti and New Zealand – would fill a medium-sized book. Such an anthology would firmly establish that surfing was indeed a very important part of day-to-day life in the middle and south Pacific Islands inhabited by the seafaring Polynesians. These accounts would also increasingly fuel speculation about surfing's origins, because despite all this recorded "oral history," nobody can quite pin down just where this maritime dance form was born. Who on this planet first meditated on the recreational use of gravity and moving-wave vectors? And who shaped the first surfboard and paddled into that first breaking wave?

There are early travel-diary accounts that describe people riding planks of wood in the surf in various parts of the world, but most surfing anthropologists, citing properly published records, defer to surfing sightings logged by the British navigator Captain James Cook in 1777. During

A Hawaiian gent on a Waikiki beach that not too many people would recognize today. What would he think of Kalakaua Avenue?

December of that year, on the occasion of his second voyage to the Pacific, Cook wrote in his ship's journal about a curious Tahitian water exercise the natives called "**choroee.**"

What Cook was witnessing, of course, was surfing, though in this first recorded incident the surfer was a lone waverider who was enthusiastically catching waves with a short outrigger canoe that he would vigorously paddle over and into incoming sea swells. This Tahitian canoe surfer, Cook observed (in Volume 11, Chapter IX of **Cook's Voyages**), was so absorbed by what he was doing that he ignored the mysterious "Western" foreigners who were watching him from Matavai Point. Noting the romance inherent in this fascinating form of recreation, Cook compared the flowing and hypnotic effects of surfing to the soothing feelings one experiences when listening to classical music.

"I could not help concluding that this man felt the most supreme pleasure while he was driven on so fast and so smoothly by the sea," Cook wrote after watching that canoe surfer negotiate several waves. Cook said that ice-skating was the only "pleasure" in England "with whose effects I could compare it."

Captain Cook's navigating and writing careers were both ended abruptly on February 14, 1779, when a group of angry natives attacked and killed him and four of his marines in the shallows of Kealakekua Bay on Hawaii's Kona coast. However, his second-in-command, Lieutenant James King, took quill in hand and described the spectacle that was surfing in Stone Age Hawaii. King notes (in Volume III of **A Voyage to the Pacific Ocean**) that in Hawaii "swimming is not only a necessary art, in which their men and women are more expert than any people we had hitherto seen, but a favourite diversion among them." About surfing, an "exercise" which "appeared to us most perilous and extraordinary," King wrote: "The boldness and address, with which we saw them perform these difficult and dangerous manoeuvres was altogether astonishing and scarcely to be credited."

Cook and King were the first but not the last author-explorers to become entranced by this "astonishing" activity. During the next hundred years and more, dozens of missionaries, adventurers and authors visited Hawaii and recorded colorful impressions of this sport.

Unfortunately for both Hawaiians and surfing, many of the first and most influential reactions to this sport were penned and spoken of by zealous Christian missionaries who found many social phenomena associated with the sport to be decidedly un-Christian. These straitlaced religionists frowned upon surfing's semi-nudity and sexual connotations, and aggressively deplored and declared to be *kapu* (taboo) the drinking, merry-making and gambling that usually took place at ancient-style surfing contests. "Immoralities"

such as surfing and hula-dancing were strongly discouraged.

Surfing also suffered from the general decimation of the Hawaiian population after the coming of *haole* (outsiders). When Cook "discovered" Hawaii it was estimated that some 300,000 native Hawaiians were living and thriving on the archipelago's six major islands. During their first century of exposure to the West, however, the long-isolated, and thus genetically weaker, Hawaiians died by the thousands of both serious and common diseases, and their race shrank in numbers to about 40,000 by the 1880s. That factor alone explains why favorite surf spots became less and less frequented during the ninteenth century.

Hiram Bingham, leader of the first party of 14 Calvinist missionaries to arrive in 1820 in Hawaii from faraway New England, wrote in 1847: "The decline and discontinuance of the use of the surfboard as civilization advances may be accounted for by the increase in modesty, industry or religion, without supposing, as some have affected to believe, that missionaries caused oppressive enactments against it." He was the same Bingham, however, who, upon arriving in Hawaii, wrote from shipside: "The appearance of destitution, degradation, and barbarism, among the chattering, and almost naked savages, whose heads and feet, and much of their sunburnt skins were bare, was appalling. Some of our number, with gushing tears, turned away from the spectacle. Others, with firmer nerve, continued their gaze, but were ready to exclaim, 'Can these be human beings?! . . . Can such things be civilized?'"

Hawaiian waveriders were facing difficult times indeed, but despite the awful decimation of their race and the supression of their ancient traditions, other, more sophisticated visitors left their islands charmed by what they saw on land and at sea.

In 1825, for example, the British sea captain George Anson Byron, master of HMS *Blonde* (and a cousin to the great poet Lord George Gordon Byron), reported that in Hawaii of the 1820s a surfboard was a very fashionable part of a young male Hawaiian's estate. "To have a neat floatboard, well-kept, and dried, is to a Sandwich Islander what a tilbury or cabriolet, or whatever light carriage may be in fashion, is to a young Englishman."

A year later the author-missionary William Ellis observed surfing and remarked, in opposition to many of his colleagues, that "to see fifty or a hundred persons riding on an immense billow, half immersed in spray and foam, for a distance of several hundreds yards together, is one of the most novel and interesting sports a foreigner can witness in the islands."

20

By the 1860s even the witty American author Mark Twain had visited Hawaii and succumbed to the siren call of the surf. In *Roughing It*, a humorous collection of Twain newspaper articles published in 1866, Twain described his first and last surfing experience. "I tried surf-bathing once, subsequently," he wrote, "but made a failure of it. I had the board placed right, and at the right moment, too; but missed the connection myself. The board struck the shore in three-quarters of a second, without any cargo, and I struck the bottom about the same time, with a couple of barrels of water in me." Like most novice surfers, Twain was greatly frustrated in his attempts to surf and could only watch in awe as a native Hawaiian, or "heathen" as he called him, came "whizzing by like a bombshell! It did not seem that a lightning express train could shoot along at a more hair-lifting speed," he exclaimed.

It was during the 1800s that there also emerged – from purely Hawaiian intellectual circles – a number of well-educated Hawaiian scholars who began recording and writing many of their people's fast-fading oral history chants. Prominent among these Hawaiians were Kepelino, Samuel Manaiakalani Kamakau (1815–76), John Papa Ii (1800–70) and David Malo (1793–1853). These four Hawaiians were not particularly interested in surfing, but in their voluminous accounts of everyday and historical Hawaiian events, the subject of surfing – in either a practical or legendary context – emerges time and again. Ii even

BISHOP MUSEUM

describes in great detail how and from what kind of indigenous woods various ancient surfboards were made, and even why board designs varied depending on what kind of wave a person wanted to ride.

In the four men's accounts, the Hawaiian word cited for surfing was *he'enalu*, and surfboards were referred to as *papa he'enalu*.

These Hawaiian historians have contributed a great trove of information for modern-day surfing historians to draw from, but despite their efforts, it wasn't until the so-called "popular press" and "name authors" began paying attention to this unusual Hawaiian athletic activity that surfing really caught the attention of the outside world. Indeed, surfing's greatest publicity push didn't take place until 1907 when the famous American author Jack London wrote a widely circulated story entitled *A Royal Sport: Surfing at Waikiki*.

London, who attempted surfing during a hol-

moting the islands' hula-dancing, music and surfing as part of a glamorous, Hawaiian-style vogue.

Also, and probably as a result of London's popular surfing story, his original "Brown Mercury," an Irish-Hawaiian Waikiki beachboy named George Freeth, was invited to the United States mainland to conduct the first-ever surfing demonstrations in Southern California. Freeth's West Coast promoters introduced him as an "aquatic attraction" and as "a man who can walk on water," and for the next 12 years he remained in California and taught dozens of would-be surfers to ride waves, Hawaiian-style, for the first time.

Freeth (1883–1919) died young – "as the result of exhaustion from strenuous rescue work" performed on California's busy beaches. On a plaque beneath a bronze bust erected in his honor next to a pier at Redondo Beach, he is identified as the "First Surfer in the United States" and as the man – of Royal Hawaiian and Irish ancestry – who "as a youngster . . . revived the lost Polynesian art of surfing while standing on a board."

Young Freeth's pioneering accomplishments – on behalf of his people and their favorite sport –

iday spent in Hawaii that summer, stood up on a moving surfboard, immediately experienced what he described as "ecstatic bliss," and as a result of this waterborne euphoria described a Waikiki surfer as a "Brown Mercury" who emerged from an "invincible roar . . . not struggling frantically in that wild movement, not buried and crushed and buffeted by those mighty monsters, but standing above them all, calm and superb, poised on the giddy summit, his feet buried in the churning foam, the salt smoke rising to his knees . . ."

London's colorful piece about surfriding is often credited with reviving Hawaiian surfing enthusiasm and stimulating overseas interest in surfing. His excitement about the sport was also picked up and supported by a new Hawaiian industry – tourism – which began extolling the virtues of exotic Hawaii in propaganda distributed throughout the world. To attract visitors, Hawaii's businessmen and government leaders began pro-

Above left: **O***n an old wooden plank you could fit anything, even your pets.* **Right***: George Freeth — truly one of surfing's great heroes — remembered with a statue in California.*

were, as Lieutenant King said more than one hundred years earlier, "astonishing," but five years after Freeth had turned California on to surfing, yet another young Hawaiian appeared on the international watersports scene, and he carried Hawaii's favorite sport to legendary heights of esteem. That man, Duke Paoa Kahanamoku, is the subject of the next chapter.

ONI   EHUKAI   KNUTE   FRED   HILO

Jude Miller.   H. Nainoa.   K. Cottrell.   F. Wilhelm.   Hilo Boys.

Kim Wai.   L. Kaupiko.   J. Hjorth.   Joe Enshaw.   H. Kahanamoku

Pua Kealoha.   Lady Langer.   E. Liebtrey.   Stubby Kru

Duke Kahanamoku

AND THE SPREAD OF SURFING

NICK CARROLL

With surfing, the Hawaiians knew they were on to something amazing. But it was something the rest of the world barely knew existed, except for quaint tales from the logbooks of the slaughtered Captain Cook's historian and the traveler's essays of Mark Twain.

It remained for the word to spread somehow. And that lot fell to Duke Kahanamoku.

Duke Paoa Kahinu Mokoe Hulikohola Kahanamoku Junior was born on August 24, 1890, one of six brothers, the son of a Honolulu police captain. It is said the Kahanamokus can trace their lineage back to Kamehameha the Great, but this royal link has nothing to do with Duke's first name. In fact the name was passed from father to son in honor of the Duke of Edinburgh, who'd visited Hawaii in the month Duke Senior was born.

By the turn of the century, surfing the long *olo* board of the ancients was a forgotten art. The arrival of the missionaries, followed by the trading barons and the pressures foisted on the Hawaiians by cash-hungry kings, had cut short the development of their greatest sport. A few people played in the Waikiki shore break on little pieces of wood about six feet (1.8 meters) long. Along the beachfront the members of the informal Waikiki Swimming Club cruised, taking out canoes, organizing swimming races and generally relaxing.

*T*his 1920s portrait of Waikiki beachgirls and beachboys includes such well-known exponents of surfing as the Duke and his brothers, and Pua Kealoha.

24

In 1907 things started happening for the few surfers at Waikiki. A man named Alexander Hume Ford decided to set up a formal surfing and canoeing club, to be known as the Outrigger Canoe Club.

Today the Outrigger is one of Waikiki's *haute kama'aina* scenes, with a restricted membership and a bar, restaurant and clubhouse on land that must be close to priceless. The original intention of Ford and his surfing colleagues, which included author Jack London, was to help kick surfriding into another gear. It worked. Later that year, after an article by London was published in the US press, Waikiki's star surfer of the day, George Freeth, was hired for surfing demonstrations in California. Thus George, the world's first pro surfer, cracked waves off Redondo Beach on behalf of the California–Redondo Railway Company.

Duke Kahanamoku was a 17-year-old kid at the time. But already he and his brothers Sam and Sargent were well known on the beach, as much for their powerful swimming as for riding waves. Duke was of medium height, very dark, quiet and keen not to offend, yet assertive and knowledgeable when it came to matters of the ocean. He joined the Outriggers for a while, but in 1911 he and several others quit and set up the Hui Nalu (literally: "surf club") in friendly opposition to the Outrigger crew, and the scene was set for some great canoe and surf races.

In the meantime, something interesting happened: around 1909 Duke introduced the 10-foot (three-meter) surfboard. The longer board was better when it came to paddling, positioning, catching waves – in fact, just about any aspect of surfriding was better on a long board. The raw material was redwood; the boards weighed anywhere from 60 to 80 pounds (27 to 36 kilograms). This brought just about every break in the Waikiki stretch within a surfer's reach, the exception being zero-break Kalahuewehe, off the outer reefs in the bigger swells. Duke, George, "Dad" Center, Dude Miller, Harold Castle and a steadily growing band of followers began to nudge surfing back into the Waikiki life. Then came the 1912 Olympic Games.

Duke was 21 when he swam in the US Olympic

time trials, after a spectacular record-smashing 100-yard (91.5 meter) dash through Honolulu Harbor had been disallowed by the absent national authorities. He qualified easily. The 1912 Games were to be held in Stockholm, and they became almost the sole preserve of Duke and a part-Indian athlete called Jim Thorpe. In Duke's first swim, the 100-meter (109-yard) heats, he broke the world record by three seconds, and from then on it was a walkover.

The Games did something for Duke that surfing alone could never have managed. He was famous. The idea of this island boy emerging from the clear Hawaiian waters to beat the world's best was almost overpoweringly romantic, and Duke's demeanor – always quiet, friendly, humble, yet

BISHOP MUSEUM

To the outside world Duke was first and foremost a champion swimmer — two gold medals, and probably robbed of a third (and the record) by the First World War. For surfers, his swimming skill is sometimes too quickly drowned in tales of his surfing prowess.

dignified – fitted the bill perfectly. Not only that, the young island boy was skilled at a sport so exotic it was almost unbelievable to many mainland Americans and Europeans.

Back he went to America, where he and Thorpe were greeted by enraptured fans and journalists. Duke swung into a round of swimming exhibitions across the country. It was only natural that, when conditions allowed, he would go surfing as well. That year, 1912, he surfed waves in Florida, Atlantic City and Corona del Mar near

Newport, California. People watched, a few of whom recalled George's Redondo show.

The fame of this all-swimming, all-surfing Duke grew and grew. He found himself in Hollywood, where he spent much of the next two decades playing bit-parts in jungle movies, nightclubbing with Johnny Weissmuller and taking some friends on surf trips to Corona. Surfing developed a tight Californian cult following.

In early 1915 Duke was invited to visit Australia, where the Freshwater Surf Club swimming crew talked him into putting on a boardriding display. It didn't take much talking. Duke made a board out of a lump of sugar pine and headed down to Freshwater, a northern Sydney beach, on a warm summer's day in February with a good six-foot (1.8 meter) swell. He surfed for five hours, at one point taking local girl Isobel Letham out for a tandem session. Claude West, a young swimmer from Manly, was the lucky kid on the spot when Duke gave away his lump of sugar pine. Claude took it away, learned to ride it and passed on what he knew to a small, devout pack of budding surfriders, among them Charles "Snow" McAlister.

Duke had sown the seed for the growth of the tallest trees in modern surfriding. Later the board ended up at Freshwater Surf Club and hung from its clubhouse wall, where years hence one of Australia's first great surfboard makers, Joe Larkin, would sneak it out for an occasional surf.

Back in Hawaii, surfing on the new 10-foot (three-meter) boards was booming. In 1910 Duke reported that only five or six surfers could ride first-break Kalahuewehe. By the summer of 1917 dozens were crowding the inside breaks at Queens and Canoes, and more of the strong and skillful were cracking first break. Then one morning a monstrous, perfect swell appeared. At 8.30 a.m. Duke and Dad Center found themselves about 500 yards (450 meters) offshore at Kalahuewehe, watching as a huge set of waves came at them. Duke estimated the waves at around 30 feet (nine meters) high. At first they thought the waves would break on them, but then they realized they were in the ideal takeoff position. Dad took the first, Duke the second, and the

Duke was a famed "ladies' man" until his heart was snared by wife Nadine. **Right**: *The poster from Duke's early visit to Australia in 1915 — another surfing seed was sown.*

Duke Paoa Kahanamoku

World's Champion Swimmer

First Appearance in Sydney

Domain Baths, Sat. 2nd Jan.

ALSO

6th and 9th January

W. W. SCOTT, Hon. Sec. N.S.W. Amateur Swimming Association
Sports Club, Hunter Street, Sydney

pair surfed their giant waves right across the face of Waikiki Bay. These were the longest rides in perhaps half a century; the kind of legendary stuff needed to build further surfing's backbone.

The United States was between wars, full of young men looking for such challenges. One was a mainland kid called Tom Blake. Surfing filled Blake with a sense of mission.

In 1920 Duke successfully defended his 100 meter title at the Antwerp Games, having been robbed of a shot at three in a row by the First World War. The Antwerp win set off another round of exhibition swims and public appearances. In Detroit he met Blake and urged him to take up swimming. Soon Blake was living on Oahu, learning to surf and watching with great interest as the next generation of surfboards, the 12-foot (3.6-meter) balsas, were brought into being by Waikiki local Lorrin Thurston.

In those early days surfboard paddling races were almost as big a deal as surfriding. Bigger, in a way, because as yet no one had managed to work out a sensible means of competing while riding a surfboard. Size of wave and length of ride were the main thrills, but how did you accurately measure either of those? Paddling was where surfers got their competitive buzz. It was the basis for the early Californian surfboard clubs, where riders like Preston "Pete" Peterson, the Vultee brothers, Whitey Harrison, Wally Burton and Bob Sides were riding their own versions of first break.

Paddling was so big that Blake, whose fascination with the surfboard pushed him to research the Hawaiian roots of the sport, decided to design a board along the lines of the ancient *olo* ridden by the Hawaiian chiefs – narrow, sleek, and 16 feet (4.8 meters) long. He added another dimension: the Blake board was hollow.

Tom Blake launched the hollow board, a prototype weighing 120 pounds (55 kilograms), at Corona del Mar Surfboard Club's 1928 paddling championships and was almost laughed off the beach. The thing was so long and narrow that after 100 yards (91.5 meters), Blake was 30 feet (nine meters) off the pace. But the board's balance and

By 1922, everyone could ride Queens break at Waikiki on the new redwood boards popularized by Duke and his buddies.

four extra feet (1.2 meters) made a huge difference. A couple of minutes later he'd overhauled the field, and jeerers had to applaud. A couple of minutes after that he hit the beach 100 yards ahead, and the hollow board was on its way.

By December 1929 he had designed one for riding at Waikiki, and gave Duke the measurements. By this time Duke, almost 40 years old and still capable of qualifying for the US Olympic water polo team, was growing bored with surfing his regular 10-foot (three-meter) board. He used Blake's measurements to craft a 16-footer (4.8 meters) of his own from redwood, and one day in 1930 finally hauled it out to Kalahuewehe. "The first big swell the Duke caught went to his head like wine," writes Blake in his book *Hawaiian Surfriders 1935*. "He yelled and shouted at the top of his voice as he rode in. It put new life into him."

The 12-footers had put first break within range. The 16-footers took the Waikiki surfers all the way. With Duke's and Blake's recommendation the hollow board took off and by 1935 there was a whole crew, from both the Outrigger and Hui Nalu clubs, waiting to ride the big waves of Kalahuewehe zero break on their big new boards.

The hollow board started something new. But in a way it was also the end of an era. Surfing had more or less climbed back to where it had been before the missionaries arrived in Hawaii, with their talk of idle sport and the need for hard work. Now it needed to take a step into the unknown.

The Second World War stalled surfing's progress. But the war would later have a potent effect on the sport, as it did on so many other human activities, by the leaps in technology that it spawned – the plastic foams and resins.

In Australia the sport was in the hands of the surf clubs, and Snow McAlister was an unusual figure on his 16-footer. The clubs had more interest in rescue work, surf swimming and the eternal surfboat races.

In the days when 75-pound (34-kilogram) boards were all the go, it helped if you were big and strong. Tom Blake was both. He was also a committed designer who brought forth the first hollow surfboards.

The Californian scene was something else. Just before the war, surfing had been on the verge of a serious boom. Blake had stuck a simple fin on the bottom of his boards – a basic adjustment that arguably made more difference in the long run than any one design idea before or since. Surfers could now turn and set a board on a line across a wave. In the late 30s this meant surf contests, boardriding clubs (Palos Verdes, near Los Angeles, being the biggest), and more and more people tackling waves. If there was a hangup, it lay in the sheer bulk of the boards, difficult to wield for anyone less than physically tough; but some boards were being made from plywood with the weight pulled down to 50 pounds (22 kilograms) or less. Pete Peterson was the dominant figure, with Loren Harrison and Dick Tucker not far behind.

In 1941 all that shut down. By the end of the war hardly anyone was surfing American coastlines. For those who returned from the war still keen, or for kids just out of school, there was only

28

one source of new boards in the whole of California – a partly crippled hydrodynamics student from Santa Monica called Bob Simmons.

Simmons had a withered arm and spent a lot of time trying to make surfing easier for himself. Together with a couple of hot young surfers, Matt Kivlin and Charles "Buzzy" Trent, he turned to the hollow-board ideas of Tom Blake, but with one crucial difference: Simmons sandwiched polystyrene foam between the wood before using the new boat technology to seal his boards with fiberglass and resin.

This colossal leap might have been even more colossal had polyurethane foam been around at the time. Styrene foam dissolves under polyester resin. That made the plywood necessary.

Simmons, with Kivlin and a Californian boat builder named Joe Quigg, kept playing with their boards. They used glass over balsa. They shaped redwood and balsa rails on to their plywood-foam models. They began shaping in the first rudiments of bottom curve. Quigg made the first foiled fiberglass fins.

In the early 50s the focus began to shift back to Hawaii, where breaks on the west and north shores were being ridden for the first time. Trent and a few other Californian kids were heading over to spend idyllic months on the beach at the west side's Makaha. In 1954 the first Makaha International surf contest was held, won by local George Downing. It became an annual event, eventually drawing surfers from as far afield as its name suggests. Surfing was on its way.

PETER LUCK PRODUCTIONS

Duke's last surf was at the age of 60, on one of the newfangled balsa boards. He'd seen surfing go from almost nothing to the edge of the big boom of the 1960s.

So Duke Kahanamoku saw the sport he'd carried to the world begin to sprout into something its ancient Hawaiian masters would never have guessed at.

Duke lived through a dignified middle age. He was voted Sheriff of Honolulu, a largely honorary position, 13 times running. He left the Sheriff's job and was made the Official Greeter for the extraordinary array of fascinated foreign big shots who by the 1950s were crowding into the Islands for a look at the hula dancers, coconut palms and surfriders. Around the late 1950s, after a series of

health problems, Duke quit surfing. In 1966 the first Duke Kahanamoku Invitational surf contest was held at Sunset Beach on Oahu's North Shore, which by now had taken the place of Kalahuewehe as the hottest surf spot in the world. Local disc jockey and entrepreneur Kimo McVay helped Duke establish a restaurant-nightclub business, which thrived into the mid-60s. Duke Kahanamoku died suddenly of a massive heart attack on January 22, 1968, next to his boat mooring at the Waikiki Yacht Club. The funeral was the biggest Hawaii has ever seen.

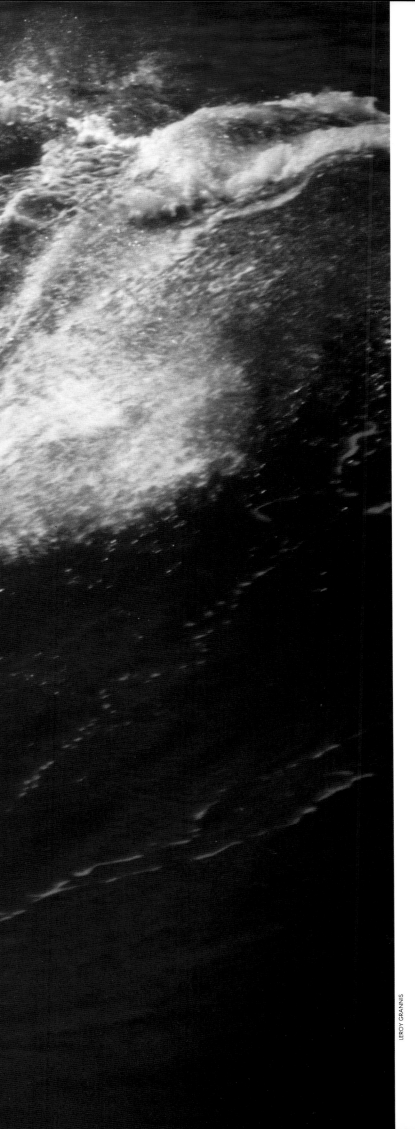

The Growth of a Sport

TIM BAKER

War and sport don't mix – particularly an indulgent sport like surfing. The early developments of the modern era in surfing virtually came to a halt during the Second World War as surfers were drafted into the armed services and the war effort took the impetus away from a pleasure-seeking pursuit.

Surfing's immediate post-war history was a period of fractured development. The sport was growing on three main fronts – California, Hawaii and the east coast of Australia – but surfers had no way of knowing what direction the sport was taking elsewhere in the world. There were no surfing magazines, no surfing movies and only the word-of-mouth of the few international travelers of the time. Nevertheless, design, performance and geographical frontiers were explored by a legion of pioneers all over the world, who all owed something to the efforts of those who had gone before them.

With peace came an end to gasoline rationing, the return of service men and women, and the emergence of a younger generation prepared to question the path their parents had mapped out for them. The same social climate that gave rise to rock and roll made the time ripe for the growth of surfing.

A healthy cross-pollination between Californian and Hawaiian surfers had been developing since the late 1940s. The true big-wave pioneers were surfers of great courage, tackling the huge

By the end of the 1950s Real Men knew where the Real Waves were breaking — Waimea Bay, Hawaii. Here Phil Edwards (on the inside) and Dan Haut take the drop on a comfortable one.

32

SATURDAY EVENING, AUGUST 4, 1928   9*

AN INVITATION
TO - YOU - OF
"Orange County"
SPEND THE DAY WITH US

AT THE

"Corona Del Mar Beaches"
ON EAST SIDE OF NEWPORT BAY

BRING YOUR PICNIC BASKETS—PLENTY OF CLEAN SAND BEACH

NEXT SUNDAY AUGUST 5th

Pacific Coast Surf
Board Championship

The Meet Is Under the Auspices of the

Famous Corona del Mar Surf Board Club

ALL ORANGE COUNTY FOLKS WILL BE THERE SUNDAY

Largest Club of this class in America. Its membership includes such world famous figures as Duke Kahanamoku, Tom Blade of Redondo, Gerrard Vultee, Art Vultee of the Los Angeles Athletic Club; Clyde Swedson, Swimming Coach to the Hollywood Athletic Club; L. Jarvis, R. Williams, H. Hutchinson and many other famous experts in Surf Board Riding.

REFEREE—Mr. L. Henry, Los Angeles Athletic Club
STARTER—Capt. T. W. Sheffield

FIRST EVENT 12:00 M.

1.—PADDLING RACE ACROSS BALBOA CHANNEL FROM CORONA DEL MAR BEACH TO JETTY AND BACK.
2.—CANOE TILTING CONTEST.
3.—DEMONSTRATION OF LIFE SAVING BY SURF BOARDS. (Members of the Club rescued fifteen men off the Thelma when she capsized in a rough surf.)
4.—THRILLING ROUGH WATER SURF BOARD RACE FROM BELL BUOY TO CHANNEL NEAREST EAST JETTY.

Prizes Donated by W. S. Sparr, H. Bowman, Balboa Palisades Club, T. W. Sheffield, The Dyas Co., Los Angeles and Hollywood

ALL ORANGE COUNTY FOLKS WILL HAVE A GOOD TIME

THE PRIZES WILL BE PRESENTED TO THE WINNERS BY MAYOR JOHNSON OF NEWPORT BEACH

Races Commence Fifteen Minutes After the First Aerial Bomb at 12:30 P. M. on the West Beach of Rocky Point, Corona del Mar. The Rough Water Surf Board Race Commences from the East Beach Following the Paddling Races.

REMEMBER——
Corona del Mar
REMEMBER——
THIS "PROGRAM" IS ABSOLUTELY FREE
THEN - TOO——

YOU WILL SEE OTHER WONDERFUL SIGHTS DURING THE DAY, SUCH AS THE SPEED BOATS "WHIZZING" BY—THE AIRSHIPS—THE SAILBOATS—THE BEAUTIFUL YACHTS GOING IN AND OUT—THE FISHERMEN WITH THEIR CATCH — THE "BATHERS" ENJOYING THE "STILL WATER" AND "SURF", THE "GROUPS" ALONG THE BEACHES, HAVING—

A WONDERFUL TIME

DIRECTIONS
FROM THE ARCHES, SOUTH, FOUR MILES TO MARGUERITE AVENUE, ON STATE HIGHWAY

What was this contest like? Corona Del Mar, 1928, the Duke, Tom Blake (his name misspelt on the poster), Aerial Bombs to start the paddling races . . . the mind boggles.

Hawaiian surf on primitive equipment and with no real knowledge of the possible consequences. The origins of the modern big-wave gun go back to 1938 and a surf session at Diamond Head, Hawaii, with three surfers in the water – Wally Froiseth, Fran Heath and John Kelly. On their crude, flat, finless, square-tail planks they were taking off on 15- to 18-foot (4.5–5.5-meter) waves and side-slipping, spinning out and generally displaying the sort of reckless bravado that typified the big-wave pioneers. In frustration, they returned home for lunch where they took to their boards with an axe and roughly fashioned the first narrowtails. That afternoon they discovered the holding properties of the narrowtail in big, steep surf. They dubbed the board the "Hot Curl" and the modern big-wave gun was born.

The war slowed down this early progress, but a surfer named Woody Brown, a conscientious objector, stayed behind and surfed and worked on boards with his friend George Downing, who was too young for the draft. Woody had been a champion glider pilot and applied his enthusiasm and knowledge of aerodynamics to surfboards. He refined rocker and rail curves in an effort to surf closer to the pocket of the wave.

After the war, Wally Froiseth and George Downing were introduced to fiberglass by Bob Simmons and admired his sandwich boards. They took their new-found knowledge back to Hawaii and experimented with lighter boards and fins. By 1958 Downing had just about perfected his fin size and placement, allowing him to ride bigger waves than ever before.

Around this time, Woody Brown virtually dropped out of surfing after a horrendous big-surf experience with his good surfing buddy Dick Cross. At a time when the limits of big-wave surfing were being pushed further with each new swell, Cross and Brown were out at Sunset Beach one day when the waves just kept getting bigger and bigger, until Sunset was closing out at 18 to 20 feet (five to six meters), and there was no way in. These days, swells are predicted with great accuracy, right down to their exact size and the time they'll hit. If

JOHN SEVERSON

surfers get themselves into trouble there are life-guards with jetskis and rescue helicopters standing by. But for Brown and Cross that day, no such help was at hand. They paddled to Waimea Bay along a stretch of coast dotted with cloudbreaks – outer reef surf spots that break miles out to sea – and must have looked on in panic and awe as the fury of the ocean erupted all around them. Eventually, Cross saw a chance to surf one of the billowing waves in at Waimea Bay. He disappeared over the ledge of the wave as Brown yelled at him not to do it. Cross drowned and Brown was found unconscious on the beach.

Despite such experiences, or perhaps partly because of the romanticism and mysticism of the big-surf tales that drifted back to the mainland, the flow of Californian surfers to Hawaii quickened throughout the 50s. Stowing away was a common means of transport and thrifty surfers became renowned for their frugal lifestyle in Hawaii – living more than a dozen to a house, eating spartan diets, sleeping on crowded floors, and surfing. Many surfers settled permanently in Hawaii, giving up careers, relationships and families to satisfy their surf lust in the world's best waves.

During the 50s Californian surfers such as Pat

From left, Henry Lim, Alfred E. Neuman, José Angel, Jack Webb and Peter Cole, November 21, 1959, Waimea Bay. A very good day for the crew. By the way, which of these names are fake?

Curren, Buzzy Trent, Fred Van Dyke, Peter Cole, Jose Angel and John Severson had moved to the Islands. In the same period, regular visitors included Phil Edwards, Micky Dora, Greg Noll and Mickey Munoz.

The prominence of big-wave riding has varied during different eras but those pioneers are remembered for literally venturing into the unknown. Greg Noll is credited with being the first surfer to surf Waimea Bay successfully, home of the world's largest rideable waves and a surf spot shrouded in mystique. Phil Edwards is widely accepted as being the first man to surf the Pipeline, a freakish, frightening wave that barrels over shallow coral and which intimidated even those hardy pioneers right through the 50s. Edwards didn't tackle it until the winter of 1960–61. No matter what other surfing trends have been in or out of favor, groundbreaking Hawaiian performance has been one of the hallmarks of almost all surfing's great champions.

The first issue of **Surfer** magazine, turned out by John Severson in 1960, was an oddly shaped creature with some of the most exciting surf shots ever taken stamped on its horizontally cut pages. **Clockwise from top**: The cover of that outlandish issue; Alan Gomes gets up to the nose; Kemp Aaberg looks for a Rincon tube; Mickey Munoz demonstrates the ``Quasimodo;'' three heroes, Munoz, Dora and Mike Doyle, cut brave figures in a ``trandem.''

34

In Australia, surfboard riding was firmly entrenched in the Surf Life Saving Association (SLSA) – a national, voluntary organization that patrolled the country's beaches. Up until the mid-1950s, surfing barely existed outside the structure of the powerful SLSA. Those few isolated pockets of surfers who existed separately were considered rebels, and surfboard riding was treated only as a fun diversion from the serious business of beach patrol and rescue. The focus of the regular surf life-saving carnivals was the surfboat race in which large, cumbersome wooden surfboats from opposing clubs would race out to sea and back to shore. In heavy seas the surfboats almost inevitably came to grief in the shore dump, though, strangely, this never led to any serious questioning of their effectiveness as a means of rescue. A position on the surfboat crew carried great status and the surf club was the social hub of any beach.

Surfing in Australia would not have progressed beyond this rigid structure so rapidly had it not been for a visit by a group of American lifeguards and a series of American surf movies. In 1956, as part of the Melbourne Olympics, the Americans came to Australia to compete with Australian life-savers and give displays of their style of surfing on their balsa surfboards. Their impact was profound. Australian surfers were riding 14- to 18-foot (four- to five-meter) hollow paddleboards and performance surfing amounted to taking off on a wave as far out to sea as possible and trying to ride it to the sand – no mean feat on the awkward equipment. The Americans, including leading surf star Tom Zahn, trimmed across the waves with a poise and agility never before seen in Australia. Their surfing displays at Manly and Avalon, in Sydney, and Torquay in Victoria, enthralled their spectators.

Surfers scrambled to ride one of the balsa

The Aussie surf club in the 50s, before boardriding took off by itself, contained the flower of Australian youth. The March Past, Queenscliff Beach.

NEWS LTD

Surf skis, designed to ride waves, were the pride of the Australian surf clubs for many years.

PETER LUCK PRODUCTIONS

36

boards (Malibus, as they became known) or to get a copy from local board builders. The fledgling Australian surfboard business could hardly cope with the demand and, as balsa was even more scarce in Australia than in America, approximate hollow replicas were produced.

Not all reaction was positive, however. Skeptical older surfers considered them a novelty, too small and light to pick up waves as far out to sea as the huge paddleboards. Newspaper articles of the time recorded either fascination at the latest "craze" ("so light that girls are riding them!" one Sydney paper trumpeted), or horror at the new menace on Australian beaches. "The problem with the new boards is that they shoot waves at an angle, across the waves, instead of straight in like the old type," Bondi's chief beach inspector Aub Laidlaw was reported as saying. "They turn almost before the rider thinks of it, and if the rider is thrown, they go anywhere on the next wave, generally toward surfers." It should be noted that by surfers Laidlaw meant swimmers or bodysurfers.

The SLSA joined the outcry, dismayed by the popularity surfboard riding was achieving, and the threat it posed to lifesaving club memberships. But when American film-maker Bud Browne's surfing movies came to Australia soon after, showing what the top American surfers were doing and capturing the magnificent waves of Hawaii, Australian surfers en masse were inspired.

The board industry blossomed, mainly in the industrial suburb of Brookvale. Manly surfer Roger Keiran was the first to build a balsa board in Australia, but the supply of balsa remained unreliable and irregular. There was still beautiful hollow construction being done, especially by Brookvale board builders Bill Clymer and Joe Larkin. Performance surfing was being pushed by surfers like Bluey Mayes at Bondi, and Dave Jackman, who conquered the feared Queenscliff bombora on a 10-foot (three-meter) balsa gun.

By 1960 the American foam and fiberglass construction had arrived, and accidents were common in the industry hub of Brookvale as Australian board builders struggled to master the new materials. Cries of, "Look out, she's gonna blow," rang out as another resin mix went wrong. Australian surfers, too, were basically copying the American model, but with Australia's mainly coastal population and great surf, it wasn't long before some wonderful natural talents emerged. A small, slightly built teenager named Bernard "Midget" Farrelly, from Manly, soon stood out head and shoulders above his peers, quickly mastering everything he saw the American surfers doing in Bud Browne's movies. In 61 Midget and a group of other Australian surfers traveled on the cruise ship *Oriana* to experience first hand what they had been hooting and yelling at on cinema screens in Australia. Australia's rise as a surfing force was under way.

With advancing designs and enhanced surfing performance, it was inevitable that competition would become more serious. But almost from its inception competitive surfing was plagued by arguments over the inherently subjective nature of judging the sport, and some of surfing's great rivalries developed around radically contrasting styles and approaches.

One of the perennial arguments in surfing history is about who was the greater surfer – Phil Edwards or Mickey Dora. The pair held sway in the Californian surfing scene through the late 50s and the 60s. Two surfers of uncanny, but totally different, natural abilities, they both emerged at a time

when the burgeoning sport was eager to adopt leaders, or its first superstars. Edwards was one of the first power surfers, wielding the big, heavy boards of the time with brute strength. Dora, lighter and more wiry, had impeccable timing, balance and placement. Between them, they placed new demands on their equipment and so advanced design as well as performance.

To the general public the "Gidget" phenomenon was the public face of surfing – the cute caricature of the Californian beach culture portrayed in the hugely successful series of *Gidget* movies in the early 60s. But to the surfing fraternity, Edwards and Dora were the source of inspiration. Formal competition was never the main focus for either surfer but they dabbled with the notion of professionalism through endorsements.

The parallels between the Dora–Edwards rivalry and Australia's first two major surf stars – Nat Young and Midget Farrelly – are uncanny. In 1962 Midget took out the unofficial world title, the Makaha contest in Hawaii, a victory that attracted a great deal of publicity back home in Australia. Robert "Nat" Young was still a gangly teenager surfing at Collaroy, on Sydney's northern beaches, showing extraordinary skill on a surfboard. Nat

PETER LUCK PRODUCTIONS

Surfing sure got into some embarrassing situations in the 1960s. Australian rock 'n' roller, Johnny O'Keefe, and his lineup of beach "bunnies."

*F*riendly rivals then — later, not so friendly. Nat Young and Midget Farrelly rinse their boards under the tap at Makaha, Hawaii.

*W*orld champs, 1964. Midget Farrelly and Phyllis O'Donnell and the spoils.

was at first something of a protégé of Midget's, carefully perfecting the Mickey Dora brand of fluid, positional surfing. As a rivalry developed and Nat sprouted to a hefty six foot two (188 cm), he developed a powerful style and following of his own, and he and Midget became fierce competitors.

The first official world championships were held at Manly Beach, Australia, in 1964. The rising popularity of surf music and Hollywood beach movies had attracted enormous interest in surfing, and the world championships drew corporate sponsorship from gasoline retailers Ampol, as well as an estimated crowd of 65,000. Midget won it in front of his home crowd, ahead of California's Mike Doyle, second, and Hawaiian Joey Cabell, third. Midget was a star and surfing was big news.

Surfing began branching out as never before, both geographically and in performance. Surfers were becoming aware of tube riding – surfing inside the hollow curl of the wave – and the sport

RON PERROTT

was growing in places as far afield as South Africa and Peru. The 1965 World Championships were held in Peru and local surfer Felipe Pomar came first, with Nat Young second.

The 1966 world titles were held in San Diego, California, where nose riding was still considered cutting-edge performance, and the wonderfully gifted David Nuuhiwa was a strong favorite to win. He would bottom turn, walk to the nose of the board and climb and drop the entire length of the wave on the nose. But the Australian contingent arrived in San Diego with a different act. Nat had been collaborating with Australian surfer/shaper Bob McTavish and the somewhat eccentric Californian kneeboarder George Greenough. Together they had come up with a design and style built around sudden, radical directional changes. Nat's board was shorter and thinner than his opponents'

Nat Young, his first step into the big time, gripping his trophy at the 1963 Australian Titles. Mick Dooley, at left, was runner-up.

and his surfing was fresh, fast and powerful compared to the nose-riding devotees.

Nat won the 66 world title and the Australians reveled in the success. "We're tops now," one surfing magazine article claimed. The collaboration between McTavish and Nat continued with the "fantastic plastic machines," still shorter, V-bottomed boards that made it easier to put the board up on its edge through turns. The trend to shorter and shorter boards and more radical directional changes gathered momentum and surfing entered what became known as the "new era." It is a sad quirk of Australia's surfing history, though, that its two early leaders remained derisive about

LEROY GRANNIS

LEROY GRANNIS

David Nuuhiwa was called the supreme noserider by many. **Top**: *He puts that theory to the test at San Clemente.* **Above**: *Victory at the US championships.*

each other's contrasting contributions to the sport. To this day Midget and Nat do not speak to one another.

The late 1960s was a confused time in surfing's history. Some still see it as a golden era of design experimentation and innovation, alternative life-styles and counter-culture consciousness. Others see it as a dark, shameful era of drug-induced design lunacy and a period in which surfing fell from grace.

Ground-breaking surfers of the period included Hawaiian Jock Sutherland, an ambidextrous surfer who set the pace in Hawaii in 67 and 68; Californian Rolf Aurness, who won the 1969–70 world title at Johanna in the tranquil countryside of southwestern Victoria, Australia; and a teenage kid from that same part of Victoria named Wayne Lynch. His vertical goofyfoot surfing was revolutionary, developed in a country backwater far from the surfing mainstream.

DEAN WILMOT

The Rise and Rise of the Pros

THE PROFESSIONAL ERA

DEREK HYND

Martin Potter's 1989 World Championship completed a remarkable 20-year cycle. Surfing's clockwork revolution – from arcane counter-culture to a vivid analog of the 90s dream: affluence combined with a bonding to nature. The profession that delivered Nat Young the promise of things to come, with a $5000 winner's purse in 1970s token pro event, the Smirnoff Pro Am, now sits atop three million dollars on the key Association of Surfing Professionals (ASP) World Tour, with a multi-billion-dollar spinoff industry as testament to its power. No small achievement.

In a generation of such rapid industrial change, the growth of professional surfing mirrors the inevitable drift towards new values. Sixties' sage Alvin Toffler perceived an enforced growth in leisure lifestyles, and dubbed surfers "the signpost to the future." His label is coming home. Technology is destroying traditional work practices. The streaks of its waste have become sources of social chaos – unemployment, insecurity and pollution have had the double effect of increasing leisure time and forcing new respect for nature and environment. The life of a globetrotting surfer simply puts him or her in the limelight.

Surfers haven't changed so much; society has. Today's hero, destined millionaire Martin Potter, looks, acts, even philosophizes, the way yesterday's hero, Nat "The Animal" Young did when he

The epitome of the modern pro — flames on his board, deck grip in place, 1989 world champion Martin Potter hurls himself down an Off-the-Wall section.

disturbed convention in the 70s. But now it's different. "Pottz," as he's widely known, is such big news that he establishes convention and influences the social habits of millions. He's so attuned to the 70s that he's cutting a throwback track. And the irony is that the surfer genre is now so well oiled and image-positive that it's self-perpetuating. Just his presence is a sponsor's reward at any one of 28 events worldwide. Fans expect personality, in or out of the surf, and often get it. Personality sells.

Take 1990's top 10 most marketable pros — Pottz, Tom Curren, Tom Carroll, Mark Occhilupo, Matt Archbold, Christian Fletcher, Richie Collins, Sunny Garcia, Brad Gerlach, and Kelly Slater. They're all diverse individuals, whether wildly extroverted, introspective, illiterate, articulate, passive, violent, happy, maddened, raised by the

family unit or raised in a city street. Because they appeal to a cross-section of the community, the surfing image strikes a common chord. Different surfers for different tastes. They attract fanatical support in every surfing nation, which keeps both big-money contest promoters and multinational clothing sponsors well satisfied. These 10 pros have been responsible for industry growth of a billion dollars, particularly in America.

By the same token, 1970's top 10 most marketable surfers – in probability, Nat Young, Midget Farrelly, Rolf Aurness, Reno Abellira, Wayne Lynch, David Nuuhiwa, Corky Carroll, Gerry Lopez, Barry Kanaiapuni and Jeff Hakman – appealed to no broad social spectrum. As part of a slowly generating industry, largely dependent on the US magazines *Surfer* and *Surfing* for exposure, surfers

DEAN WILMOT

*The intense competition on today's world tour means that even the warmup sessions are spectacular. **Opposite**: Mark Occhilupo wrenches a high top turn. **Above**: Richie Collins gets even higher — did he make it?*

were stereotyped as draft-dodging, acid-dropping, subversive hippies. There was no chance of even a mini-boom along the lines of fledgling pro tennis. Mother Nature, and a lot of soul, meant far more to these surfers than a material life of birth, school, work, death; and society could not relate to surfing's alternative lifestyle.

Had conditions been right, the personalities were there to be exploited. And the quietest of them all could have been as powerful a hero as the latter-day Tom Curren. The 1970 world champion, American Rolf Aurness (son of actor James Arness), was a lot like Curren in both demeanor and talents. Yet soon after his brilliant win at Johanna, Victoria, in Australia, he quit surfing to pursue musical endeavors. Had Curren been of the same era, I daresay he would've done something similar. It was simple. Once at the top, Aurness saw no amazing career path.

Runner-up to Aurness, Midget Farrelly, wasn't surprised by the champion's break. "Politicking was so strong that it detracted from the whole thing," Midget says. "People with no empathy for the ocean, driven by politics, were running the show. The 1966 and 1968 World Titles were marred events, and 1970 was wonderful because Rolf came through. But he saw the politicking as going nowhere. He turned his back on the sport and started playing the piano. At the same point, I

Left: *The wizard of the early 1970s, Michael Peterson.* *Opposite:* *Tom Carroll treats a Pipeline drop with professional calm.* *Inset:* *Carroll and Curren — the two greats of the 1980s.*

thought 'There's no future here.' The public image wasn't good because of perverted results, and characters at the fore. I couldn't see it getting better, only worse. I couldn't see any money coming into it. I gave up.''

Then, in the 1970s, Mark Warren, Peter Townend and Ian Cairns formed a daring promotions outfit called ''The Bronzed Aussies.'' This attempt at improving the public image of surfing, backed by the media, was eventually successful.

Overseas, the mood was still a stagnant bog of apathy. American surfing was very much locked in the post-60s void, with competitive pursuits a low priority. The Japanese market was in, at best, an early fad stage. And Europe's potential remained unsighted and untapped. International competition came from South Africa and Hawaii, with both nations offering the Australian leg of the International Professional Surfing (IPS) circuit an attractive meld of gregarious characters. The likes of Shaun and Michael Tomson, Reno Abellira, Larry Bertlemann, Dane Kealoha, Michael Ho, Mark Liddell and Montgomery ''Buttons'' Kaluhiokalani, took on locals Wayne Bartholomew, Mark Richards, the ''Bronzed Aussies,'' Simon Anderson,

Terry Fitzgerald, Col Smith and Ron Ford. Today's pros enjoy impressive international kudos and believe their standard to be far superior to the embryonic IPS days . . . but they're sadly mistaken. The year 1977 was one of nonconformist approaches – from the speed lines of Fitzgerald, to the ''radical'' aggression of ''Gentle Giant'' Anderson, to the past vertical attack of Smith, to the layback cutbacks of Townend, to the swooping power of Richards, to the incredible 360-degree turns of the young Hawaiians and, saving three masters of esthetic tube riding till last – Bartholomew, Shaun Tomson, and the one, the only, Michael Peterson. Surfing was more vibrant, and it needed to be.

This was the keystone year of the pro era. Visionary Peter Drouyn rose from the ashes of a checkered 13-year career to smash convention. At the inaugural Stubbies Classic in March 1977, he introduced man-on-man competition, with ''anything goes'' rules, designed to intensify the battle aspect. It was high-risk gambling from John Phillips, marketing head of Stubbies Ltd. Gone was the confusion of six-man heats; gone were competition vests, replaced by Stubbies red or yellow

THE BRONZED AUSSIES

DEREK HYND

PETER CRAWFORD

Two young surfers approached Midget Farrelly one day in the early 70s and said, "What can we do to make surfing as popular as it was in the early 60s?" Their names were Mark Warren and Peter Townend. The advice was: "Make the public love you. If you build public image, you have to control it – prevent what happened to the surfing machine as the 60s wore on." In 1976, along with Ian Cairns, they formed a daring promotions outfit, the "Bronzed Aussies," and set about revolutionizing surfer credibility.

But it was no welcome revolution. The media-targeted venture was incredibly abrasive to surfing's purists. There was, however, a climate for acceptance amongst youth. The Rip Curl Bells Beach Easter Classic, the 2SM Coca-Cola Surfabout and the Alan Oke Memorial brought reactionary barbs from the "soul" side of surfing, which was still the dominant force. Advocates of the new style, often wearing luminous wetsuits in the lineup, attracted streams of abuse and accusations that the lifestyle was prostituting itself. The Bronzed Aussies pushed "Glam Surfing," and the ensuing backlash forced every surfer to decide just how he or she wanted to be perceived.

Since 1972, attitudes had been changing. Michael Peterson, Mark Richards, Wayne Bartholomew, Simon Anderson, Terry Fitzgerald, Paul Neilson, Townend, Warren and Cairns became state-of-the-art. And while their lifestyles still embraced the counter-culture, the aggression of a new surfing was obvious.

PETER CRAWFORD

With the introduction of "Bronzer" and "Stinger" surfboards worldwide, experimentation with faster, looser techniques became an option. The kid at the beach saw the shift, whether photographically, in the major magazines, or in the flesh. The early decision had to be made: "Do I want to stay laid back and local, or copy the latest styles?"

The issue was further compounded by the advent of legropes. The device originated in the United States (which was still locked in the past), and was vehemently rejected for several years. "Kooks" wore the cords, and were ridiculed. Good surfers saw the users as wimps in need of assistance. Yet, in the end, the sheer practicality of the legrope won out. The twin-fin, particularly in Australia, was another design

breakthrough that led many teenagers to take up the challenge of surfing far faster than before. The gap in age attitudes widened. By the time the Bronzed Aussies shocked the old guard, thousands of surfers had already left soul surfing in search of something new.

By 1977 several factors gave "the BAs" a lot of room to move: journalist Graham Cassidy's success in promoting the 2SM Coca-Cola Surfabout since 1974; Australia's growing dominance in giant Hawaiian surf; a groundbreaking film, *Free Ride*, which romanticized the talents of three future world champions, Shaun Tomson, Wayne Bartholomew and Mark Richards; and Peter Townend's inaugural world professional title, in 1976. The ensuing media push was a loud, hard sell – Townend, world champion; Ian Cairns, the circuit's

Opposite top and bottom: Peter *Townend's cunning and commitment helped make pro surfing work — and he didn't do a bad job surfing, either.* **A**bove: Ian Cairns, *shown here behind Mark Richards at Waimea, gave a generation of young Americans a big boost with his Californian scholastic surfing efforts.*

leading purse winner and world champion; Mark Warren, Smirnoff pro champion. Orchestrated by Sydney journalist Mike Hurst, it was at times crass and transparent, with the three articulate, courageous Bronzed Aussie sportsmen making public appearances in velvet jumpsuits. But the message was nonetheless received. Australia accepted surfing's new image, at a time when world champions and incredibly brave sportsmen were at a premium.

board shorts. It was conflict, a test of mind and body, with heroes and villains for spectators to respond to. And, crucially, it was 1977's opening event. Failure meant a massive setback. As fate would have it, the waves at Burleigh Heads, Queensland in Australia, were some of the best in the history of competition. It was undoubtedly the small-wave contest of the 70s – won by local folk hero Michael Peterson. Victory by this unkempt, antisocial symbol of the Gold Coast lifestyle in no way detracted from pro surfing's improving image. So perfect was the TV footage that living-room Australia was humbled by this dolphin-like mastery of nature. "MP's" bad habits were forgotten amidst the euphoria, and the IPS prepared to introduce Drouyn's system to 70 percent of the world tour.

Image building wasn't limited to the seasoned pros. Youngster Tommy Carroll arrived at Burleigh with a load of kudos. This protégé of Col Smith had weeks earlier come from nowhere to win the inaugural Golden Breed Junior Pro, for the under-19s at North Narrabeen, on Sydney's northern beaches. This important event gave voice to surfing's youth movement, and victory became symbolic of career destiny. Parents first realized that teenage surfing wasn't without reward – Carroll was just 15 years old and had captured international reputation in one swift hit. As a showcase of the Next Generation, the Pro Junior remains today a promoter's dream. Hawaiian teenage sensation Sunny Garcia still has no qualms about calling it "the most important event in the world, more important than the OP Pro" . . . Victory has eluded him.

The year 1977 also provided pro surfing with a mainstream television outlet. David Hill, a producer with Australia's Channel Nine, put together the first in a series of award-winning documentaries on the 2SM Coca-Cola Surfabout. It still rates today as a masterpiece of sports production, utilizing aspects of state-of-the-art land, water, and aerial photography. Local powerhouse Simon Anderson won from the trials, repeating his Rip Curl Bells Beach Easter Classic win the week before. Many labeled him "the world's best" at the

DEAN WILMOT

time. It was a moot point in relation to his presence in front of a crowd, or camera. He was certainly king of the public speakers; the driest, wittiest, most spontaneous character in the game, and the media didn't mind a bit.

South African all-rounder Shaun Tomson took the world title by winning the World Cup at Sunset Beach, Hawaii. The series of Australian developments had made opportunities for pro surfing, but public appeal lay in footage of surfers battling terrifying Hawaiian waves. These men and women were no egg-shelled athletes trapped in a court, or strolling round a course. It was obvious, even to American "Wide World of Sports" viewers, that these people confronted fear and pain, even death, in eking out their existences. Tomson was a superb spokesman – the classical world champion – articulate, nonchalantly brave, confident, exotically spoken, fine looking. And he attracted

important people. By the end of his reign the profession had enough foundation on which to build in America and Japan, with sufficient fresh personality to stimulate interest in contests and sponsor products. Come the next world champ, there was enough gloss laid over the past few years to allow a wild man room to blow minds without blowing the sport out the door. The marketplace reacted — favorably.

Wayne "Bugs Muhammad" Bartholomew won the 1978 World Title. And his sponsors, Quiksilver clothing and Rip Curl Wetsuits (both located in Torquay, Victoria), eyed America. Not since Hang Ten clothing rode round America on the back of maestro Phil Edwards's image, in the early to mid-60s, had a surfer's reputation been exploited so sweetly. It was the dawn of America's multi billion-dollar surfing market. Bugs saw himself as a rock star type . . . and Americans wanted to be rock star

Three surfers took center stage as pro surfing took off — Shaun Tomson, Wayne "Rabbit" Bartholomew and Mark Richards. **Above**: *Shaun plays with his favorite wave, Off-the-Wall.* **Right**: *The master competitors, MR and "Rabbit."*

PETER CRAWFORD

types. A beautiful marriage between buyer and seller ensued, and after Bugs the same companies used young Gary Elkerton to further their thrusts. Japan also accepted the same stars as role models, and although the fad boomed, overseas companies suffered at the hands of smart operators who basically ripped many of them off in the course of two or three years. But, regardless, by 1979 the

JEFF HORNBAKER

TONY NOLAN

*In 1986 the Americans took over with two great surfers, one woman, one man. **Top**: Tom Curren cruises through a French tube. **Above**: Frieda Zamba throws her board onto a rail at the BHP Pro, Newcastle, Australia.*

Japanese leg of the IPS World Tour hosted four of the 13 events, and there was little doubt that so long as surfing's machine continued to churn out the heroes, their market would grow. Idolatries, even in this primitive stage, fanned from Shonan Beach to central Tokyo to the outer islands.

By 1982 other surfers' achievements had evolved the right climate for pro surfing's success: the Herculean achievements of 1979, 1980 and 1981 world champion Mark Richards; the ceaseless rivalry between Richards and gifted upstart Cheyne Horan; Hawaiian Dane Keoloha's powerful presence; Michael Tomson's successful American launch of Gotcha clothing; cousin Shaun Tomson's figurehead partnership in Instinct sportswear; ex-"Bronzed Aussies" Ian Cairns and Peter Townend's development of America's National Scholastic Surfing Association (NSSA) as a designer step to IPS competition; goofyfooted Larry Blair's astounding rags to riches arrogance in winning the Surfabout and Pipeline Masters (twice) in perfect conditions; Simon Anderson's revolutionary "Thruster" three-finned surfboard which delivered power off the bottom turn while maintaining speed off the top turn; Anderson's stunning 1981 Thruster debut, winning in Waimea Bay-sized surf at the Bells Beach Easter Pro, then the next week at the Surfabout, then in heroic circumstances at the Pipeline Masters.

The watershed came in September 1982. Ocean Pacific clothing, a massive success story throughout coastal America, swung boots and all behind pro surfing. Hawaiian Larry Bertleman had been its promoted surfer through the mid- to late 70s, but focus shifted to the NSSA team . . . and Tom Curren. NSSA director Cairns set up the OP Pro beside the famed Huntington Beach Pier and let the tens of thousands of spectators do the rest. In an amphitheater atmosphere, Curren's pro debut unfurled to tumultuous reception. His fifth place could easily have been victory, had he been dealt any luck. The top professionals were stunned by his meld of composure, savvy, and wave utilization. One thing was certain: America had found its hero. The very next event, the important Japanese Marui Pro, was his all the way. Even without saturation advertising, Tom Curren's electricity spread by word of mouth. He *would* be world pro champion. It seemed obvious.

Cairns altered the structure of the profession, replacing Hawaiian Randy Rarick's seven-year-old IPS ruling body with the Association of Surfing Professionals (ASP), basing it in the heartland of big money – Orange County, California. His vision also focused on the new age of a Tom Curren world championship, perceiving a lifestyle boom.

The rise of Curren was the pro era's most powerful tool. And, importantly, it was no easy road. Richards captured an incredible fourth world title, denying Horan for the fourth time, and that's where their dynasty ended. Curren, South African wonderboy Martin Potter, and Tom Carroll were the future. Had it remained that way, the industry takeoff still would have happened – the scenario looked like a dream international faceoff. But a

JOLI

Through the 1980s, one surfer was the focus of more amazement, amusement, pity, curiosity and disdain than any other. Then in late 1989 he won the richest surfing contest in the world and everybody fell silent. Cheyne Horan.

DEAN WILMOT

was the highest in the sport, relative to any era. Curren caught his level, somehow elevating himself each time. Pros like Martin Potter hit the mark in free surfing, but not in competition. And both Carroll and Elkerton took to big Hawaiian surf in a similar groundbreaking foray. But the crowds, particularly at the OP Pro, came to see the Curren–Occhilupo contests. Possibly the greatest 60 seconds in the modern game occurred after Occhilupo's fifth, and Curren's sixth, ride in the 1986 OP Pro semifinals. They raced, neck and neck, in a frantic bid to be the first to reach the priority buoy (which determined right of way), with the Australian needing to win in order to mount a last ditch, final wave comeback. Sixty thousand American fans went berserk in the desperate mêlée. Occhilupo won the race, then selected the winning ride. An hour later a bloody riot erupted, which made headlines round the world.

Ocean Pacific conquered the Middle American market thanks to Curren; Billabong clothing broke into coastal America on the reputation of its boy, Occhilupo; Gotcha clothing roamed throughout on the basis of brilliant advertising portrayals of its boy, Potter; then Quiksilver Europe took advantage of a stagnation in Continental windsurfing by pushing the Carroll image as a beach-life alternative to still-water sailing, and exploiting the value of Curren's alternative lifestyle in France.

Through Curren's 1985 and 1986 world championships, Damien Hardman's of 1987, Barton Lynch's of 1988, Martin Potter's of 1989, and both Carroll and Elkerton's domination in Hawaii, there's now a youth movement throughout the expanding Western world, reacting to the styles and attitudes of surfing's role models. Increasingly, surfers stand as symbols of achievement through harmony with nature, and the ASP world tour carries the message.

powderkeg catalyst was still round the corner.

The 1983 ASP tour featured 16 events worth $US350,000 compared to the 1976 IPS tour of 12 events worth $US65,000. It also bred controversy because of the title race's Australian finish, as opposed to the former's Hawaiian finish. Several Hawaiians revolted, and were penalized. But the Cairns ploy paid dividends. Tour prize money doubled in two years, and tripled in five.

The super growth was a direct result of the interest generated by the plainly awesome battles between Tom Curren and Mark Occhilupo, from June 1984 to April 1986. While not detracting from the achievements of master surfer, 1983 and 1984 world champion Tom Carroll, who redefined the criteria of pocket-power surfing and sacrificed a 1985 title by boycotting two South African events, Curren and Occhilupo turned Drouyn's man-on-man dream into reality. First two, then four, then eight ferocious wave-for-wave showdowns, where the standard of excellence lifted every time. The pinnacle; a rivalry that may never be matched, or even approached. The mark reached by Occhilupo

Today's pro is a dedicated athlete with near-perfect surfing style — clumsiness just isn't permitted, in or out of the water. Above: Barton Lynch swoops at Rocky Point. Opposite top: Damien Hardman's compact aggression at Narrabeen. Opposite below: Gary Elkerton puts all his power into a fin-cracking bottom turn at Off-the-Wall.

A World
of Surfing

Pipeline, one of the top testing
places for endurance and skill,
roars into action for a
hungry surfer.
Inset: A high-angled turn from
Gary Clisby.

California

LAND OF SUN, SAND AND SURF

SAM GEORGE

Mile for mile, wave for wave, long sunny day for day, no coastline in the world packs as much diverse surfing energy into its boundaries as that of California, America's Golden State.

Eight hundred and forty miles. It's hard to believe that the stretch of shore that has come to define surfing and beach culture the world over makes up such an insignificant contribution to the global map; even more incredible is the influence those 840 miles (1350 kilometers) have had on worldwide fashion, music . . . and attitude. But packed in between its boundaries – Mexico to the south and Oregon to the north – is a surfing culture that has become so multi-faceted that it exemplifies the modern spirit of the sport.

Sure the sport of Hawaiian kings has taken off worldwide, with the Sandwich Isles still the ancestral home of the first wave-riders. Australia is the number one surfing power; Europe is crazy about the sunburned, salty and sandy-toed set. Yet it is in the California Experience that the mystique of surfing becomes the most accessible, because nowhere else is the experience so richly varied.

Malibu's long, sunny walls of Surfers Point are so crowded in the summer there's hardly room to park your Porsche. Farther up the coast in Del Norte County, a surfer paddles out at the Klamath Rivermouth, alone save for a few Indians salmon fishing with dip-nets nearby.

At the OP Pro championships in Huntington Beach, 120,000 spectators jam the pier and crowd the beach to watch favorites like Tom Curren and

Blond-haired California Kid, Kevin Billy, aims a sleek backhand turn down the wave that many have come to recognize as typical of the Sunshine State — Salt Creek.

HANK

Mark Occhilupo do battle for thousands of dollars and pro ratings points.

Eight hours north, the only crowds at Ano Nuevo in Santa Cruz are the elephant seals who colonize this beach that features a clean summer peak.

The boardwalk at Newport Beach is an endless parade of beach fashion and beach bodies, tanned to a golden brown. In Mendocino, north of the

solitary surf sessions before heading back to the mainland with their catch.

The California coast has oil derricks and grass shacks, beachfront condos and towering coastal redwoods, long white sand beaches and foreboding rocky cliffs. Along this coast break waves of every imaginable size, shape and style, from the thundering 15-foot (4.5-meter) walls of Steamer Lane to the gentle rollers at Bolsa Chica. On these

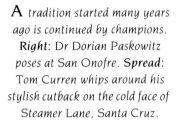

JEFF DIVINE

A *tradition started many years ago is continued by champions.* **Right**: *Dr Dorian Paskowitz poses at San Onofre.* **Spread**: *Tom Curren whips around his stylish cutback on the cold face of Steamer Lane, Santa Cruz.*

Golden Gate Bridge, surfers struggle out of quarter-inch-thick wetsuits and crawl into wool sweaters and parkas.

Cruise down to Hermosa Beach and it seems that the entire surfing population is under 16; the line-ups pulse to the beat of hot-and-cold-running hormones.

At San Onofre, a silver-haired grandfather sits outside the breaker line waiting for another set, a living relic of those distant days when boards were made of wood and men of iron.

Orange County boasts the greatest concentration of surfboard manufacturers on earth – and a large portion of the industry's surfwear companies as well. Here, surfing is big business and many former beach bums now have their fun, fun, fun in BMWs.

Off Santa Barbara's Channel Islands, lonely abalone and sea-urchin divers tie up their boats for

60

waves ride surfers unlike those anywhere else. Kids, students, girls and guys, executives and hippies, pros and cons. They ride on modern thrusters and old-fashioned longboards, on boogie boards, in boats, at the beach – even in the pool – and every one of them, each time they paddle out, becomes a brightly colored piece in a mosaic that the world accepts as the face of surfing, perhaps the heart and soul as well.

Oddly enough, the "fun-fun-fun-two-girls-for-every-boy-Surf-City-USA" image that most people associate with surfing in California is more the product of canny marketing than an accurate reflection of the culture. Surfing has quite a history here, much older than the "Surfin' 60s" era that has provided the sport with its most durable stereotypes. In fact, the first wave was ridden back in 1907 by George Freeth, an Irish-Hawaiian

GUY FINLAY

MALIBU

SAM GEORGE

Malibu – what can you say about a beach town whose most famous beachboy is Larry ''JR'' Hagman? About a curious little creekmouth beach whose social scene launched the entire surfing craze that swept the country in the early 1960s? About a former Chumash Indian village that today is some of the highest-priced coastal real estate in the world?

For most of America – the world, for that matter – Malibu is the beach.

Not so long ago, Malibu Beach was merely part of a huge coastal cattle ranch, the deed having been acquired from Spanish landholders by California's Rindge family. Before that, the Chumash Indians who lived along its shore fished for abalone and hunted sea otters – before Jesuit missionaries wiped them out with disease and religion in the 1800s. However, it wasn't until some time in the 1940s that some adventurous surfer (nobody's quite sure just who)

headed north on the Pacific Coast Highway and discovered every hot-dogger's dream.

There were plenty of good beaches to hang out on in the old days, plenty of stretches of sand on which to approximate the Waikiki beachboy's lifestyle. But Malibu had not only sun and sand, it had also surf – perfect, peeling, point surf. Clean, even, summer south-swell walls upon whose watery faces was developed the mechanics of modern surfing. Top surfers, having designed special ''Malibu'' boards, took the sport out of its posing he-man era and launched the age of performance; Malibu is where the sliding stopped and the riding began.

And so they all came to Malibu, in a trickle, at first, then in hordes. The best – Bob Simmons, Matt Kivlin, Joe Quigg, Les Williams, Mickey Dora, Lance Carson, Johnny Fain, Dewey Weber, J. Riddle, George Trafton, Allen Sarlo and Willy Morris.

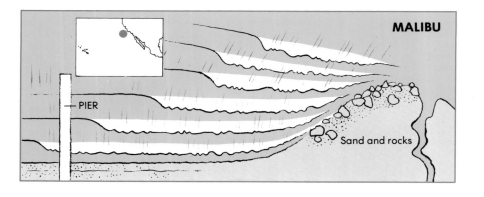

MALIBU

PIER

Sand and rocks

PETER BROUILLET

A multitude of pilgrims arrived, eagerly searching for a shrine on which to prostrate themselves in humble tribute to the laid-back surfing way of life. As the bodies piled up, pushing out the pure devotees, competition for space, as well as recognition, came at a premium. You still had to earn your spot in the lineup – the rest of Malibu went up for sale to the highest bidder. And, unlike the south swells that seemed to have waned under the onslaught, there have been no shortage of these.

Once, a surfer went to Malibu to find

The mystique of Malibu — a much-vaunted thing. Is it alive today, or smothered beneath fast food and filthy-rich movie stars? **Spread**: *Scott Daley slices his own piece of the action.* **Right**: *Malibu, mid-1960s. A warm summer's day, a nice little swell . . .* **Below**: *two of the point's most famous characters, Johnny Fain (ducking) and Mickey Dora, play havoc with each other in a 1965 surf contest.*

the perfect wave. Today, he or she can't find parking. Driving along the high-rent Coast Highway, forget about not seeing the forest for the trees – you can't even see the water. The county has taken over the beach, the rich have taken over the berm and the kooks rule the water. Billboards advertise Malibu cigarettes, while Malibu Barbie spearheads an anti-animal-fur campaign.

And in the cool of a moonlit summer night, waves roll in from the Pacific and peel towards shore, unseen, unridden, lapping upon Malibu's shore and gracing its tired cheek with the magic kiss that once, so long ago, created the very mystique responsible for Malibu's tragic demise.

RINCON POINT

THE CURRENT STATE OF AFFAIRS AT THE LITTLE CORNER-BY-THE-SEA

MATT GEORGE

Rinconada-del-mar (Spanish: "little-corner-by-the-sea") is Californian surfing's heartland. Neatly placed on the coast near Santa Barbara, the long, winding point break has been ridden for over six decades.

Down beachfront, all tarry driftwoods and sandstone cobbles, a blushing pink horizon is the only light for the dawn patrol. At this hour, it's always a potpourri in the lineup. Mostly quick-draw artists on a frantic mission before school or work. A plumber, a contractor, a college freshman and his little brother, a boogie boarder, a mat rider and some guy on one of Greenough's old spoons. While everyone is still moving into their respective positions, some 16-year-old kid takes off on a screamer and lucks into the fastest moment of his life . . .

"Rincon? I think it's an overly crowded, great break. It's hard to get waves when there's three guys to one.

That's why I dawn it whenever I can talk my dad into it . . .

"I don't feel that special about Rincon yet. Maybe I'll feel different when I grow up, but right now, it's a lot of work . . ."

JAMIE GEORGE, 16
YEARS SURFING RINCON: 3

A couple of guys are sitting up on the sea wall. Every kind of surfcraft and its owner will eventually trot by. From guys in ragged beavertails arming old Yater spoons, to the kids in neon wetsuits with their nitro-burning funny boards.

The boys on the sea wall spot something and stand up for a better view. Outside, a familiar figure has started his run from way back. And by the time he hits his third bottom turn, Rincon has given its favorite mascot all the room in the world . . .

"I definitely feel when I go out at Rincon that it's my home break . . . but I can't ever see it becoming a hotbed of talent. It's just not in the nature of the place. Sure, it's crowded, but I don't mind so much. You always find ways around it, pay your dues . . . it's worth it."

TOM CURREN, 25
YEARS SURFING RINCON: 18

BRIAN HUGHES

Up at the top of the point, as far back as you can take off, a tribunal of the older surfers sits patiently. Suddenly a big set lumbers in, intent on scattering the troops. On the beach, two female surfers have just arrived and they shade their eyes to look out and gauge the size of the swell. They are just in time to see their shaper plummet down into the shadow of an eight-foot (2.4-meter) outside bowl and square a mean bottom turn. The girls watch as he leans out for speed, standing tall . . .

"It's the guys that ride it all the way through that ride it properly. Our crew looks down the line knowing that there's more to come . . . I think that is what this wave is all about. I often wonder if the younger guys feel the way we do about

Rincon. I think that our era is the last, as far as Rincon being a life's blood sort of thing . . ."

MATT MOORE, 36

YEARS SURFING RINCON: 25

Dusk. An earnestness has seized the lineup. Everyone wants their last wave to be a beauty. The walls are now dark humps, almost foreboding, nobody really wants to wipe out in the twilight's last gleaming. Of course the end-of-the-day-monster-set steamrolls in. As the last strength of a hundred limbs scratch for the shoulder, five shadows take off tightly bunched. Three pull back, one

Rincon has never had the big Surf City wraps of Malibu, but most surfers know where they'd rather ride. Opposite: a coastal curve.

pearls up to his knees, and the last one standing is some old man wearing a water-polo cap, hurtling along on an 11-foot (three-meter) tandem board . . .

"Rincon will always be here, long after we are all through with it. Some kid once said to me out in the lineup 'You know, mister, this is all going to catch up with you some day.' And I just said, 'Well, son, that may be so . . . but it hasn't caught me yet . . .' "

"SNODGRASS," 74

YEARS SURFING RINCON: 57

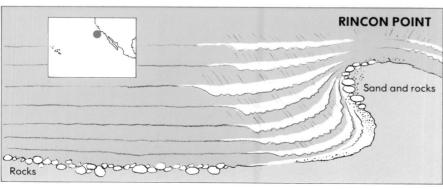

RINCON POINT

Sand and rocks

Rocks

LEROY GRANNIS

Two great surfers of the same era, who took different styles and made them work. **Right**: *Corky Carroll, the manic hotdogger, 1966.* **Below**: *A man whose name spells relaxed grace for his San Diego friends, Skip Frye.*

66

beachboy who was flown over to the mainland by a land developer interested in promoting a new trolley line. Freeth's surfing exhibitions up and down the coast of Southern California thrilled thousands and inspired a whole new wave of sportswear. Small, tight-knit factions sprang up in beach towns like Long Beach, Palos Verdes, Hermosa Beach and San Clemente. Riding their crude, wooden boards, these intrepid watermen reveled in the clean, uncrowded waves and pristine coastline. By the 1950s dozens of surf clubs proliferated throughout the state, as more and

more rideable breaks were discovered. Surfers were a unique tribe, non-conformists who saw no need to embrace the growing regimentation in American society, but chose rather to live their lives to the time of the tide and wind, the beat of the swell.

Then a simple movie called **Gidget** came out and blew the whole thing wide open. Adapted from a Fredrick Kohner book of the same name, it chronicled his teenage daughter's fascination with this new breed of American male – the surfer. Set on the beach at Malibu, it gave the country its first mainstream look at these new Bohemians, and a fad was born. Overnight, everyone wanted to be a surfer "just like those cats in California."

The Beach Boys, a band from Hawthorne, California, pumped out a hit called "Surfin' USA" and all hell broke loose along the previously sleepy coast.

Surfboard sales skyrocketed, with early designers like Hobie Alter and Dale Velzy moving out from their garages and into gleaming showrooms – an industry was born. Where once carloads of surfers would range up and down the Coast Highway like nineteenth-century mountain-

LEROY GRANNIS

PETER BROUILLET

men in the Rockies, now hordes of enthusiasts flocked to get in on the hippest new score around. Fashion, music, commercialism – surfing in California started it all.

In Hawaii, Kanakas still showed off for the tourists as they had for almost a century. Down Under, the watersport-conscious Aussies still associated surfing with the lifesaving movement. It was in California that the entire surfing scene was developed, to the point where it became hard to distinguish where surfing's culture left off and the state's indigenous culture began. The rest of the country – the world – looked on in wonder at this

HANK

*Two great surfers, again of the same era, again making different styles work. *A*bove: Richie Collins, master of the crazy off-the-lip. *L*eft: Brad Gerlach — he looks radical, and he is!*

HANK

new free-and-easy way of life. To them, California became a place where life really was a beach, the summers were endless and the sunsets always golden.

Despite the fact that surfing in California has changed so much in the last 30 years – it now boasts over one million active participants, is home of the bulk of a billion-dollar beach-fashion industry and nearly all of its manufacturing – those durable images of old still represent the common view of what surfing is like here: surfer girls, guys in their Woody stationwagons, the Beach Boys crooning: "Catch a wave and you're sitting on top of the world."

BILL SHARP

Southern California, summertime — is there anywhere else where summer means more? Above: Mike Estrada puts in time at the photo studio, Lower Trestles. Left: Newport Beach, where the whole thing erupts.

In reality, surfing in California bears little resemblance to its postcard promotion. For the most part, the coast is rocky and rough, some of the most rugged in the continental US, and girls in bikinis are rare – one's more likely to run into a sea lion than a New Wave Gidget. Except for a 200-mile (320-kilometer) stretch south of Point Conception, the coast is relatively undeveloped and the surfing population spread out through a series of small towns strung along Highway One.

California surfing is cold. Only in Los Angeles, Orange County and San Diego does the water temperature merit riding without a wetsuit – and then only for a couple of weeks in the hottest summer months. The rest of the state's surfers shiver year-round in full wetsuits and booties, the average water temperature hovering around a chilly 55°F (13°C). During the spring, when the strong, predominant northwest winds blow, coastal upwellings can drop the thermometer into the upper forties; north of the Golden Gate Bridge, the sea occasionally heats up to a balmy 50°F.

Surfing's glamorous image, so intrinsically linked with Hollywood over the years, is also largely inaccurate. At Malibu, the stray starlet might be spotted on the sand; popular bikini contests can often lure curvaceous beauties up off the beach. But the average California surfers usually find themselves sharing the scene with dolphins, otters, whales, seals and the odd toothy predator (the area from Tomales Point, north of San Francisco, to Point Sur, to the south, is known as the Red Triangle, the white-shark attack capital of the world).

Still, the male California surfer is the archetype of the Western man. In today's society, he is the cowboy on a fiberglass mount, the individualist who traveled as far west as he could – away from the crowded, cold cities and fields – and then went one step further into the very surf that kept the rest of the continent at bay. He is the ultimate Forty-niner, ranging up and down the coast, laying claim to liquid fields of gold. He is the epitome of heart-throbs everywhere – tanned, muscular, blond-haired and half-naked.

In California the surfer has found a home. The adventure starts on the Mexican–American border, approximately 20 miles (32 kilometers) south of San Diego. Although many of San Diego's surfers make regular runs across the international frontier to sample the fine surf of northern Baja, California surfing starts in the town of Imperial Beach. This area features miles of uncrowded beach-break surf and an enthusiastic crew who considers itself separate from the rest of San Diego, to the north.

THE WEDGE

BILL SHARP

Human meddling with the ocean environment is usually cursed by surfers. But in the case of a California surf spot known as the Wedge, a little seaside development actually produced one of the world's most amazing waves.

From its first use in 1870 through the 1920s, the entrance to the harbor at Newport Beach gave ships' captains fits with its shifting sandbars and nasty shallows. After one too many deadly maritime disasters, the city fathers approved a series of improvements, the first major step being the lengthening of the west jetty. Unexpectedly, this produced a mad cauldron of whitewater next to the jetty, and this nearly chewed a new entrance to the bay right through the tiny resort cottages of the Balboa Peninsula. Sand dredged from the harbor refilled the area in 1935, creating a wide, beautiful beach which was a nice, safe place from which to watch the crazy, man-eating waves.

It wasn't until the 1950s, after the invention of the swimfin, that bodysurfers were able to seriously seize on the possibilities presented by the break. After it was featured in the classic surf film *Endless Summer*, the Wedge became a world-famous celebrity among surf spots.

The blame for the reason why the Wedge breaks in such an attractively savage manner can be pinned on several factors. Although most people tend to think of California as facing the west, along this stretch the coastline takes a bit of an inward curve and the beaches face almost due south. This orientation offers the Wedge unobstructed exposure to summer swells hurled across the equator from intense storms leaping up from Antarctic regions below New Zealand, some 7000 miles (11,500 kilometers) away. And from time to time a hurricane off Mexico will spin off thick bands of swell energy which take direct aim on the south-facing beaches.

The Wedge then adds its uniquely massive punch from a process known in physics books as reflection. As the first wave of a set makes its way along the jetty heading for the shore, a solid chunk of the wave's energy bounces off the rocks and heads upcoast where it meshes with the next wave. This incestuous marriage of forces can nearly double the size and energy of the wave as it explodes across a shallow sand bottom sometimes just yards off the beach. The swell direction, the interval between the waves and the level of the tide all work together to create a work of oceanic art ranging from perfect peaks to horrendous closeouts.

The Wedge has been called a freak show, a liquid nightmare, an ugly shorebreak and worse, and it's all probably true. But despite the colorful descriptions, the fact remains that from May to October, California's biggest waves are found (and dutifully ridden) at this peculiar little corner of beach and granite. Who's ridden the biggest wave

Is this utter madness? Two reckless adventurers take to the air and the sea at the same time. The Wedge sure doesn't muck around.

is an honor that none of the local crew really seems to want to bestow or accept. How big the biggest waves have been is easier to guess, with photos scaling out in excess of 25 to 30 feet (7.5–9 meters) on the face.

And all this because a few thousand rocks were dumped into the ocean just so – this was one wave of change that worked out just fine.

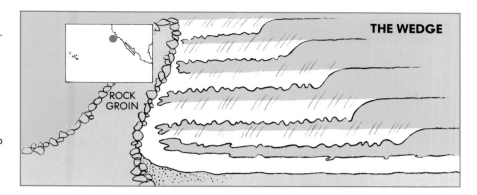

THE WEDGE

ROCK GROIN

RON ROMANOSKY

If you're running dry on waves in Southern California, well, it's only a dash to the Mexican border. Here Chris Mauro places himself well inside a beautiful wave south of the border.
Inset: Rob Bain slashes a solid cutback at the same spot.

JEFF HORNBAKER

San Diego is an old surf town with a rich heritage. Great surfing beaches abound; Windansea, a consistent reef break in La Jolla, was home to many of early California's greatest surfers – the grass shack that still stands on the beach there today is testimony to the pioneering visits Windansea surfers took to Hawaii in the 1950s. La Jolla Shores and Blacks Beach have also been a hotbed of talent over the years – Pat Curren, Mike Diffenderfer, Butch Van Artsdalen, Skip Frye, Mike Hynson, Tony Staples, Richard Kenvin, David

JEFF HORNBAKER

*O*ne good thing about Mexico — there's always heaps of time. **A**bove: Fishing keeps the coast alive. **Opposite top**: Sometimes Aussies find themselves down there too. Stuart Cadden hits it hard. **Opposite bottom**: Taking it easy before a certain tube ride.

Eggers, Peter King. San Diego surfstars are known for both their talent on a board and for having a certain panache. San Diego has always been the home of style.

Continuing north on the Pacific Coast Highway with a full tank of gas and plenty of time, a surfari would pass through the rustic beach towns of Del Mar, Solana Beach, Leucadia and Encinitas. These are sleepy little beach burgs, where Amtrak's Coastal Starlight train drops off visitors next to the railroad tracks downtown and every road leads to the sand. And at the bottom of every street, you'll find a group of locals who swears by its little half-block of heaven, talking up the days of great surf past and riding out flat spells with the sublime complacency that comes with lifelong familiarity.

Carlsbad and Oceanside are a bit more fast-paced. The waves off Carlsbad's warm water jetty

(where a hydroelectric plant pumps out jacuzzi-like conditions all year long) have spawned one of the hottest packs of surfers on the coast, and names like David and Paul Barr, Chuy Reyna and Mike Baron represent state-of-the-art performance on much more than a local level. Oceanside talent is just as rich, owing much to the consistency of the waves off its harbor jetties and piers. Joey Buran, a former Pipeline Master, and Mike Lambresi, a two-time Professional Surfing Association of America (PSAA) champion, are two of Oceanside's top guns, although 30 years before them Phil Edwards, still considered by many to be the best surfer ever, first wet his feet in the curls off Oceanside Pier.

The next major surfing site is San Onofre, where the tradition of early California surfriding lives on in the generations of families who spend

TODOS SANTOS

BILL SHARP

For California surfers, a strange and wonderful "discovery" took place in the mid-1980s – there was a surf break on an island eight miles (12 kilometers) off the coast of Baja California, Mexico, 60 miles (95 kilometers) south of the border of the USA, where gigantic waves broke in the winter. These were the sort of waves usually seen only in Hawaii. Maybe ten or twelve times a season, giant waves were there for the taking.

Of course, these waves have been breaking off the Islas de Todos Santos since the beginning of time. And true, unprepared surfers had occasionally chanced into freakishly large waves at Todos since the 1960s, but it wasn't until surf forecasting advanced to the point where accurate predictions could be made that surfers were able to organize trips out specifically to attack the big ones.

A number of surf magazine articles quickly spread the word about what waited off the "Killers" reef. It was fairly easy to get to; just an hour's drive south of the border and then a 40-minute ride in a rented outboard skiff. In fact it was *too* easy – the next season saw record crowds, but also record numbers of surfers getting caught inside, taking horrible wipeouts, realizing their surfboards and courage were too short, and deciding that maybe they weren't too interested in waves quite so big.

But for those with the skill and courage, the Todos challenge soon became an annual winter obsession. And none was affected more than Mike Parsons, one of the top-rated California surfers on the pro tour who quickly established himself as the main over-

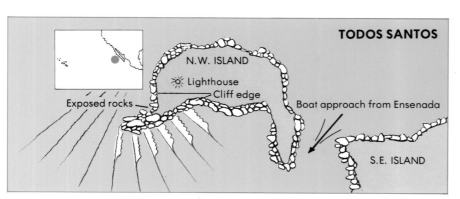

TODOS SANTOS

N.W. ISLAND

☀ Lighthouse
— Cliff edge

Exposed rocks

Boat approach from Ensenada

S.E. ISLAND

achiever at Baja's big-wave Mecca. Parsons started the decade of the 1990s holding the record for the biggest waves ridden off the island, a couple of well-documented north swell boomers a good five or six times taller than his six-foot (182 cm) frame.

The flip side of this honor is that Parsons is well qualified to describe the sensations that go along with *not* making

You want to be a big tough surfer? Pack your wetsuit, your biggest board, your longest leash and head on out to Todos and see if you can catch one of these monsters.
Opposite: the lip jumps out at you fast.
Below: Allen Sarlo pushes hard to make it off the bottom.

one of those monumental drops at Todos.

"The worst wipeout I ever had was on the really big day in February 1990," he recalls. "I got to the bottom of this huge wave and the lip came down about a foot behind my board and it just blew me into the air, like thirty feet out. Then came the hold-down . . . it was easily the longest of my life, like traveling half a football field underwater . . ."

The comparisons between Todos Santos and Oahu's Waimea Bay are too obvious to ignore. The spots even favor the same north swell direction, which means one strong storm in the Gulf of Alaska can blast Waimea with a hell-swell and then, two days later, the same bands of energy can move on 2200 miles

(3500 kilometers) to hit the reef at Todos. Hawaiian Brock Little and photographer Aaron Chang were the first to pull off what could become a jet-set trend for the future: catching a swell at the Bay, hopping a plane and catching the swell again as it arrives at the West Coast's equivalent.

In a number of ways, Todos is more dangerous than its Hawaiian counterpart. There are no lifeguards. There are no rescue helicopters. The water is cold. Medical help could be hours away. And stories of massive outside clean-up sets get scarier and scarier each year. Things to think about as you scratch for the biggest wave of your life.

BILL SHARP

PETER BROUILLET

*Two faces of the legendary Huntington Pier. **Top**: Weighed down by the burden of America's biggest pro event, the OP Pro. **Above**: Weighed down by something altogether heavier — a winter storm swell.*

the summer on its warm, sandy beach. A popular surfari destination since the 1930s, greybeards slide along next to neon neophytes in the gentle, rolling swells of this premier beginner's break.

Quite a different scene prevails at Trestles, a mile to the north. The three distinct, rivermouth point breaks make this area seethe with high-energy surfing every time a south swell rears its head. Located on a large military base and once considered strictly off-limits, this surfing reserve is now open to the public. A main attraction for a large number of Orange County surfers, the long, peeling rights and lefts prove a tantalizing treat to those surfers tired of the short, snappy beach breaks of Newport and Huntington Beach.

Huntington Beach, in fact, was once known as "Surf City USA." It has been the veritable capital of Californian surfing since the early 1960s, and hosted the United States Surfing Championships for over 10 years. The waves that peel around its famous pier are probably best known as the venue for the renowned OP Pro Championships, a major pro event that, each summer, attracts the world's top pros and hundreds of thousands of surfing enthusiasts.

But old HB has fallen on hard times. The pier has been condemned and the plethora of funky surf shops that made up its beachfront have been razed in favor of a trendy, downtown shopping complex. Nonetheless, every morning the surfers emerge from the inland housing tracts and lay claim to the best bargains in town; the appeal of Huntington Beach's sandbars will never change.

Continuing up the coast one finds pockets of surf energy in towns like Seal Beach and snooty, upper-crust aficionados in the affluent Palos Verdes Peninsula, but the next epicenter is a 15-mile (24-kilometer) crescent stretch of sand known as the South Bay. Redondo, Hermosa, Manhattan, El Porto – every street leads to the beach along this shore, where the sun, sand and surf permeate into the very lifestyle of the community. With its scenic strand and accessible beach breaks, the South Bay best represents the stereotypical California exist- ence, where tan-lines are still a status symbol and eyebrows stay salty all year long.

The Santa Monica coastline is where the Cali- fornia dream meets the ultimate dream machine: Hollywood by the Sea. From Muscle Beach in Venice to the high-rent berms of Malibu, this is the California the world knows and loves to emulate – the world of flashy women, flashy cars and long,

cool rides that last all summer. In reality, the surf is rather sparse along this coast, with Topanga and Malibu Point tottering under the brunt of a massive beach-going population.

From Malibu north to Point Conception, the California coastline begins to change, becoming less developed. Ventura features some of the state's best-shaped beach breaks, as well as aggressive, overprotective locals who have kept the area one of the least exposed. Santa Barbara, snuggled in the very crook of Conception, is the home of some of the state's best waves – period. Rincon, El Capitan, the Ranch – the list of perfect point breaks matches that of the fabled Gold Coast of Australia. Combined with a temperate, Mediterranean climate, it has all the makings of

79

There's always a hot new face in the water at Salt Creek, like Kasey Curtis, for instance, a kid with plenty of potential.

HANK

paradise, except that the mild weather comes at the expense of consistent surf; virtually all major swells are blocked by offshore channel islands, the presence of which keeps Santa Barbara surfers clenching their teeth in frustration at what could be some of the richest surfing real estate on earth.

Rounding Point Conception, the California surfer enters a completely different realm. Gone are the sunny beaches, palm trees and bikinis. They are replaced by bitterly cold water, relentless northwest winds and mile after mile of empty, unspoiled coastline. There is surf for the taking, along what is called the Central Coast, though while surf shops and surf scenes punctuate this sleepy coastline in towns like Pismo Beach, Morro Bay and Cayucos, for the most part sea otters and sea lions patrol these beaches, not lifeguard jeeps.

The region of rugged shoreline known as Big Sur is generally regarded as the most scenic in America, with its rolling Santa Lucia mountains tumbling steeply into the raging Pacific. Maintaining Highway One through this precipitous route is a full-time job, but savvy surfers have scoured every inch of the road, and a car pulled off to the side sporting surf racks usually means another isolated secret spot has been discovered.

The capital of Northern California surfing is the town of Santa Cruz, nestled into the lee of Monterey Bay. Here, a surfer traveling up the coast finds a home again, complete with surf shops, board manufacturers and clean, quality (and often overcrowded) waves. Breaks like Steamer Lane off Lighthouse Point have become legendary among California surfers, not only for their scenic nature

80

PETER BROUILLET

HANK

Surprisingly for a place so renowned for sunshine and summertime, California is often chilly for a surfer. Opposite: Peter Townend clings to a deep Huntington tube ride. Above: Santa Cruz boy Marcel Soros wonders what lies ahead on this crisp winter's day.

but also for their big waves; Santa Cruz is positioned to take the brunt of large northwesterly swells that charge down out of the North Pacific. Go big or go home, they say here, and big-wave hellmen like Vince Collier, Anthony Ruffo and Richard Schmidt achieve local-hero status every time big water starts rolling around the point. Schmidt has recently garnered plenty of international acclaim as well, doffing his 5 mm full wetsuit and making a name for himself in Hawaii, where he is considered California's top blue-water hunter.

Pass the Santa Cruz city limits heading to San Francisco, however, and the state of surfing in California takes on a whole new face – usually some shade of blue. At latitude 37° north, the sea rarely warms up past the 55°F mark (13°C) and although the coastline sports plenty of consistent – sometimes too consistent – surf, the cold water and rugged coastal conditions maintain the sport only for the most hardy and dedicated. You'll find them

scouring the redwood and fog-shrouded shore up through Mendocino, Humbolt and Del Norte counties, with the same single-mindedness that characterizes surfers elsewhere in the state. Up here, however, down jackets outnumber neon boardshorts; when the Beach Boys crooned "fun, fun, fun" some 25 years earlier, they'd obviously never pulled themselves out of the surf at Crescent City, hypothermic and shivering, with numb, frozen fingers struggling to undo stubborn zippers and car doors.

Surfing in Northern California is as far removed from the trendy, social atmosphere of its southern cousin as it would be in Kansas. And yet, in its unique way it is as much a part of the California surfing scene as drop-ins at First Point Malibu. Surfing anywhere in California is still an adventure. Adventure is what lured brave sportsmen to the surf in the first place back in the early days, and it still does. In fact, in today's crowded, over-commercialized and developed society, it might take more courage to be a surfer than ever before. But surf they do, from Mexico to Oregon, and, in so doing, they exuberantly express the very nature of the sport. Totally stoked – California surfers invented the word.

The US East Coast

MITCH VARNES

The East Coast has always been somewhat of a black sheep in the United States surfing family. Often inconsistent, mostly small and always unpredictable, the eastern seaboard is tolerated but frowned upon as the least respectable or successful of the fold – and the fold includes the likes of California, the Caribbean and Hawaii.

Almost every major East Coast surfing spot can, with the right conditions, be near-epic, but the East's most reliable power zone sits near the middle of the coastline in the agriculturally dependent state of North Carolina. Cape Hatteras and the slew of other outer banks of North Carolina jut more than 60 miles (96 kilometers) into the Atlantic, forming a chain of largely desolate barrier islands accessible only by boat or very long waterway bridges.

Driving and searching are the never-ending story of the Hatteras surfing experience because of the seashore's continuously shifting sandbars. Sand bottoms, which are perfect and near all-time one day, may be too deep or shallow the next thanks to a littoral current that steadily rushes along the ocean floor. This certain uncertainty of never knowing where the best break may be is what keeps surfers scouring over the dunes of the East Coast's most popular surfing destination, but its powerful waves and the relative assurance of rideable surf are what brings them back year after year.

*F*lorida's surf isn't hero-worshiped the way Californian or Hawaiian waves are, but the surfers seem to rise above all that. Here, Kelly Slater crashes a lip in his home town.

PETER BROUILLET

83

Summers mean near-flatness to much of the East Coast, and the air and water of Hatteras winters are brutally cold. Fall and spring, however, are an idyllic time to be at Hatteras; a time when temperatures are pleasant, and chest-high and larger waves can be surfed nearly every day.

Perhaps the best wave of the East Coast sits just offshore at the Hatteras Lighthouse, where a series of groins was constructed to dampen beach erosion. Unhindered Atlantic swells routinely roll in and ricochet off these groins, creating powerful and steep water cylinders that typically wrap for 50 yards (45 meters) or more. For over two decades surfing's largest member organization, the Eastern Surfing Association, has held its annual championships here, qualifying the lighthouse as home to most of East Coast surfing's greatest competitive moments. The lighthouse is the Outer Banks' most famous surfing beach, but other dumping sandbar breaks like America Street, Avon Pier, Frisco, Nags Head and Rodanthe Pier regularly go into a class of their own. The isolated locale of the lighthouse and all Outer Banks surfing spots has added immensely to the allure of the Cape Hatteras experience and kept it a qualified first on the "must-go" list of practically every East Coast grommet.

*East Coast surfers know the meaning and the value of travel — from Cape Hatteras, **above**, where perfect waves find sandbars up and down the coast, to Sebastian Inlet, where surfers like Matt Kechele take hot surfing to the limits.*

HANK

A couple of hours north of Hatteras is the vacation town of Virginia Beach, Virginia – a carnival-like community which arguably boasts the East Coast's largest single-point surfing population. Scores of mediocre surfing breaks dot the Virginia Beach strip, but it is again a human-made object that creates the town's best surfing break. The harbor jetty is the city's most reliable wave and the peak where Wes Laine, one of the East's most successful contemporary professionals, honed his skills before venturing onto the Association of Surfing Professionals (ASP) World Tour. Now settled at home with his family, Laine is a former member of the ASP Top 16 Club and the hero of all Virginia Beach locals.

Typically frigid ocean temperatures account for a thinning of the surfing ranks north of Virginia, but there are still plenty of high quality – and mostly empty – surfing areas up the eastern shore. Ocean City, Maryland, and the pebble-bottomed beaches off Long Island, New York, are virtually abandoned during winter but in summer attract

Scott McCranels pops his red head up all over the world, but he's never happier than when he's bottom-turning at Reef Road.

large numbers of closet city surfers from Washington, DC, and the Big Apple. Summertime waves in these parts are usually knee- to waist-high dribblers with the occasional exception of Montauk, a ritzy resort town at the southeastern tip of Long Island.

During the latter half of the 80s, New Jersey received more than its share of negative publicity concerning beach and water pollution problems. Much of it was well deserved, but officials have since jumped hoops to clean the shores and New Jersey's tarnished image. Manasquan Inlet is home to the most crowded and highest-quality break in New Jersey. A pyramid-shaped wave that peaks and splits, Manasquan has long been a hotbed for up-and-coming New Jersey grommets. Dean Randazzo is the latest and most prolific of these and a regular threat in Professional Surfing Association of America (PSAA) tour events. Randazzo and

There's only one surfer in the world who's won four world pro titles with a break in between — only one who comes back to the tour whenever she feels like it and wins a contest each time. She's a goofyfoot and she comes from Florida — Frieda Zamba.

other New Jersey area surfers have long headed up to Point Judith, Rhode Island, for point waves that on a good day match those of anywhere in the world. Point Judith is but the beginning of perfect and picturesque headlands which continue north through New Hampshire, Maine and into Canada. Water temperatures which are usually around 35°F (1.7°C) and rarely exceed 55°F (13°C), are New

England's big detractor and one of the primary reasons why many of mainland America's most incredible waves go unridden every day. A second reason is relatively easy accessibility to the warm water and good surf south of Cape Hatteras.

With several populous cities and over 200 miles (320 kilometers) of surfable coastline available, Florida undoubtedly has the highest surfing

TOM DUGAN

population anywhere on the East Coast. Except for Laine, Rick Rasmussen and maybe a couple of others, every major East Coast talent has originated from the Sunshine State. Claude Codgen, Jeff Crawford, Greg Loehr, Gary Propper and Mike Tabeling were some of the biggest names of the 60s and 70s, while others like Lisa Andersen, Todd Holland, Matt Kechele, Charlie Kuhn, Kelly Slater and Frieda Zamba are still making their marks in international competitions. A pleasant climate and amply consistent swells lure wave riders to the water more easily than anywhere else, but it's – like everywhere on the East Coast – the vast number of human-made structures that are responsible for Florida's best waves. Rock and reef breaks are scarce to nonexistent in Florida so outside of jetties

DOUG WATERS

DOUG WATERS

*Two surfers attack Florida's Reef Road. **Top**: Rich Rudolph —
the man who stayed at home and won an ASP world pro-am title.
Bottom: Charlie Kuhn — the man who went away and earned
an international reputation.*

and piers the State offers little more than rolling
sand-bottomed beach breaks.

Sebastian Inlet is one of these jetties and
Florida's most famous surfing spot. Its tubular and
dumping peaks are the daily stomping grounds of
Kechele, Kuhn, the Slater brothers, Danny
Melhado, and heaps of other Central Florida hopefuls. When the Inlet is firing so is Spanish House,
a half-mile- (800-meter-) wide sandbar just a short
distance north of Sebastian. Spanish House is not
quite as hollow as the Inlet, but it's a much shiftier
wave and can consequently support many more
surfers in the water. A little further north on the
Florida coast are other notable surfing breaks like
Shark Pit, Boardwalk, Second Light, Ormond
Beach, Mayport Poles and the State's quintessential
reef break, RC's.

Sebastian Inlet may be Florida's hottest wave,
but the surf adjacent to the New Smyrna Beach
Inlet is, if anything, just a step behind. Smyrna
could very easily be the East Coast's best summertime spot because it rarely ever goes flat. The

ocean can be lake-like all along the eastern shore, but at Smyrna there's practically always a waist-high wave to be found.

The majority of Florida spots break pretty much the same on either north, south or easterly swells. The exceptions to this rule are the beaches about 70 miles (110 kilometers) south of Sebastian Inlet, which the offshore chain of Bahama Islands blocks from receiving anything but northerly swells. Lake Worth Pier, Miami Beach, Palm Beach Inlet, Pump House and Reef Road are the better-known South Florida surfing beaches, but together they break less than a couple of dozen times each year. Arctic low-pressure systems that deliver nightmare-like snowstorms to Mid-America and New England are the weather patterns of dreams for South Florida wave riders. Such hellish storms often completely bypass north and central Florida but squeak through the door separating the Bahamas from South Florida. When this occurs at Reef Road, few other waves in mainland America can match its power and tenacity. Former ASP competitors Dave Kennedy and Scott McCranels are the two best-known South Florida surfers and both count their many Reef Road days as essential stepping stones on their path to surfing the big waves of Hawaii, Indonesia and Western Australia successfully.

Florida and the East Coast can and do get all-time surf, but are really little more than fun surfing arenas and rarely rate as pleasure travel destinations to anyone other than fellow Easterners. Perhaps it is a feeling of frustration or a genuine belief that the waves are always better across the country, just down the road or on a nearby Caribbean island that makes East Coasters among the most well-traveled surfers in the world. Whatever it is, there is also a sense of optimism in every East Coaster that is not so frequently found in surfers from more consistent locales; a conviction that the waves of tomorrow might just be better than those of today.

Kelly Slater, Florida's hot young kid in the late 80s, slaps a Sebastian Inlet lip

TOM DUGAN

DOUG WATERS

THE CARIBBEAN

MITCH VARNES

The Caribbean basin is internationally renowned for balmy weather, carefree living, limbo-dancing and reggae music; in the surfing world it's the Atlantic Ocean's passport to Mecca. Hundreds of islands and about 750,000 square miles (1.9 million square kilometers) of ocean

span this tropical oasis that starts with the chain of Bahama Banks — 50 miles (80 kilometers) off the south Florida coast — and sprinkles southward to the isle of Trinidad, just above the northern coast of South America.

Surfers have long frequented the region's dynamic reef breaks, but the Caribbean's incredibly diverse cultures — including inhabitants of African, British, Dutch, French and Spanish descent — and a multitude of quality surfing spots make each experience seem like a fresh discovery.

Puerto Rico hosted the 1968 and 1988 World Amateur Championships and is probably the most internationally famous surfing island in the Caribbean. However, hurricanes, tropical storms and even the slightest variation in the local weather system can transform the transparent waters of any Caribbean island into picturesque and appealing playgrounds. A fine example of this is Abaco's Elbow Cay, a geographically minor link in the chain of Bahama islands. A summertime hotbed for skindivers, Elbow Cay perks up for surfers with the passage of southerly squalls or the northerly cold fronts of winter. Elbow Cay's most intense break is Rush Reef, a

Far left: *When Puerto Rican sandbar waves start firing, you could be forgiven for thinking you were in Australia, Hawaii, California or wherever waves and surfing are hot. Here Scott Bouchard goes into action.* **Below**: *Doesn't this make you want to go to Barbados?*

crushing righthander that works best in double overhead-sized surf. Other consistent spots include Gus's, Garbonzo's, Japs and Indicators, the wave that may be the hollowest in the Bahamas. Scores of mostly desolate high-quality waves can be found throughout the Bahamas, but the majority require a sailboat and a good deal of time and searching to uncover — the dividends, though, can well surpass the investment.

Cat Island, Eleuthera and San Salvador are other consistent northerly islands, but the juiciest Carib surf lies in its central and southern pockets. The Dominican Republic is an economic surfing bonanza, where inexpensive lodging and meals can be obtained along the wave-rich southeast coast. Reef breaks and even a spattering of beach breaks abound in this Spanish-speaking nation, which has only recently become a surfing destination.

The neighboring island of Puerto Rico has long been a warm-water refuge for winter surfers. A window-like span in the Caribbean island chain and one of the Atlantic's deepest trenches enable the northerly swells of winter to storm unhindered onto Puerto Rico's northwest coast. Jobos, Middles, Secret Spot, Surfers Beach, Wilderness and scads of other spots are great in surf, ranging from two to 12 feet (0.6 to 3.7 meters), but the remote break of Tres Palmas is the only one that easily handles double and triple overhead-sized surf. A powerful and long right that breaks about a half-mile (800 meters) from the beach, Tres Palmas is a focal point — for both surfers and waves — for the Caribbean's biggest winter swells.

Anegada, Guadeloupe, Tortola and Trinidad and Tobago are among the southern Caribbean's best surfing islands, but each rarely receives the type of wave action that Barbados does. Barbados's extreme southeasterly location enables it to receive swells from all possible angles. During the summer months local surfers revel in the frequent south swells that roll in from Africa and

Europe, and in winter the Barbados coast is almost constantly blasted by huge North American-spawned cold fronts. The hollowest and most treacherous wave is Soup Bowls, a righthander that on a good day rivals many of Hawaii's better breaks. Brandon's, Duppies, High Rock, Maycock and South Point are other paramount surfing spots, but on a good day a fun wave can be found at almost any beach.

For the typical tourist the Caribbean is a melting pot brimming with all types of exotic culture and history. For surfers it is all that and more — a warm-water oasis regularly laden with some of the world's widest variety of waves.

*What do you want out of a wave? Want to get vertical like Rich Rudolph, **left**? What about a floater like Juan Ashton, **far left**? Or maybe just a full-blooded foam bounce like Justin Carver, **below**? Whatever, Caribbean surf gives you the green light.*

DOUG WATERS

DOUG WATERS

MARTIN TULLEMANS

Australia

WHERE THE ACTION IS

NICK CARROLL

How do you explain Australia's impact on the surfing world? We have facts, there is no shortage of facts. Australia is a country where three million people are regular beachgoers and a million of them have some kind of surfcraft. Where over 300 schools have weekly surfing programs. A country where 15,000 miles (24,000 kilometers) of surf coastline stretches in huge arcs from the Indian to the Pacific oceans, from desert to rainforest, sand to cliff to coral, where waves of almost any imaginable kind can be ridden. It is the home of half the world champions in the past 30 years and all but two in the past 10, and where the two most important surfboard designs in history were invented.

But these are raw facts, and nothing can live on facts alone. The true tale of Australian surfers and surfing is out there, if you look. Where is the beating heart of Australian surfing?

Might it be in Byron Bay? Byron, 60 miles (96 kilometers) from the Queensland–New South Wales border, Australia's easterly landfall poking its jewel-green nose out into the Pacific, sniffing for surf. Byron Bay – haunt of hippies and wild surfers in the 60s, designer holiday town in the 90s.

But the surfers survive here, riding the small clean waves as they've done for 30 years. Like Bob McTavish.

McTavish, quietly shaping his surfboards amid the hills of the New South Wales north coast, was the silent partner behind a surfing movement that wrenched the sport into the modern era. In 1967,

Aggressive yet elegant, powerful yet precise, and a lot of very good backhand work — these are just a few hallmarks of Australian surfing. Mark Occhilupo lets Burleigh have it, right in the teeth.

NEWS LTD

Midget Farrelly showed the way for a whole wave of Australian kids in the early 60s with his great win in the 1964 World Title at Manly.

96

with Nat Young as his surfer and Midget Farrelly as friendly shaping rival, he carved feet off the length of the surfboard in a matter of weeks. In six months surfing went from a trim, elegant pastime to a gouging spree of shortboard maneuvers.

Bob is a short, powerful, calm character who renounced competition, later turned Jehovah's Witness and burned his shaping notebook to cast out his "ego." "It was really a stupid thing to do," he says now, good-humoredly.

He started surfing at Caloundra, Queensland, in 1954, at the age of ten. This was before the light-weight fiberglass boards had even come close to Australian waters. Like Midget, he learned without anyone to teach him. His heroes, for lack of any-one else on a board, were surf-club board pad-dlers. He saw Midget and immediately changed his hero rankings.

Bob took to the road in search of waves. Those were days, the early 60s, when there were still waves to be discovered all the way up and down the east coast, and there were hardly any surfers at all.

"We knew every surfer from Caloundra to Cronulla," McTavish remembers. "We knew who the Bells Beach guys were because they'd come up every month or so for a visit. Surfers had a real camaraderie. We waved to anyone who had a board on the roof. Sometimes we'd pull over and stop and talk for hours."

Of course they were all characters. There were his mates Natch, Ugg and Bobcat from Maroubra, Sydney, who stowed away to Hawaii on a cruise ship because they couldn't afford the fare. There were the exploding surfboard factories in Brookvale, Sydney, as crazy surfers tried to mix the new resins together. There were fights with the surf-club guys who hated the "surfies" with a passion. But there were also some extremely tal-ented surfers. Nat Young was one of them. "I always thought Nat was unreal," Bob says. "I thought he was the most raw talent of that era. But he was never a hero to me, you know?" Bob was three years older than Nat and already a keen shaper when they began surfing together at Lennox Head, New South Wales, in the mid-60s. Up there with them was an odd little character from Santa Barbara, California, by the name of George Greenough.

The surfboards they came up with – along with Midget, who was busily hacking chunks off *his* boards every week or so – totally changed the face of surfing.

Suddenly surfboards weren't lumbering big beasts, hard to carry, difficult to turn, hideously dangerous when flying loose through the breakers. Suddenly there was a style of surfing – hard, aggressive, brilliantly extroverted – that would come to be known as pure Australian. Nat went on to become what people call an "elder statesman." McTavish had a brief taste of fame and disliked it intensely. He still lives quietly at Byron, watching his own kids learning to ride waves. "They surf the local backbeach and I know all their friends," he says gently. "I suppose I've got a certain position with 'em. I'm the old guy who first started surfing the point. But I've got no desire for glory."

Might it be in Sydney? Sydney has the glory all right. Sydney is where the glory is earned and has been for generations, glory being the sort of thing that lit up the ozone back in 1965 when someone like Dave Jackman rode Queenscliff Bombie for the first time, or Bob Pike and a couple of the boys paddled out from Manly on a big day and took a run down to Long Reef to catch a wave on the German Bank well offshore, and the cops would chase them down there and try to make them come in for fear they'd drown. Or the glory of Midget's world title at Manly Beach in 1964, and the mayor telling everyone what great boys and girls these surfers were, not crazy young swine after all.

Or, years later, Tom Carroll and Cheyne Horan at 15 years of age, surfing in tiny schoolboy contests as if a world title were at stake. Or Pam Burridge rearranging women's surfing for two generations. Sydney is competitive enough to have cranked out five world champs, and when Martin Potter was looking for somewhere to turn his talents into winnings, he picked Sydney as the training ground.

TONY NOLAN

*A lot of people still gasp when they see this man walk a board.
Nat Young, Newcastle Beach, 1989.*

But wherever or whoever you are in Sydney, there is someone ready to take you down a peg or two – as the grommets at Narrabeen have found on occasion. Narrabeen is a good, honest, working-class suburb that somehow found itself on the richest stretch of beaches in the country. The north end, with its lagoon flowout and point break, is as dependable a surf spot as the east coast can boast. In the early 1970s it was the local beach for perhaps more great surfers than have ever been gathered together before or since.

Two Narrabeen boys – Simon Anderson and Mark Warren – came as close to a world title as you can get without winning one. Two – Anderson and Terry Fitzgerald – made the surfer-shaper immortal listings. Others were immortalized in other ways: Maurie "Pig of Steel" Fleming, "Fatty Al" Hunt, "Wiggo" and Brian "Wilbur the Worm" Witty, who somehow persuaded a hapless landlord to rent them a house right on the beach and renamed it The Ghetto. Grant "Dappa" Oliver, who came third in a big contest in Hawaii then went to Wagga Wagga in outback New South Wales to play Rugby League football. Col Smith, a superbly reckless surfer and former racing driver who later shaped a young Tom Carroll his first high-performance boards.

The Northy boys were Australian heroes who played footy, went to the pub and surfed sensationally when their spot was on. And through it all their most famous invention stood, tall and proud and alone, in the middle of the Northy carpark, daring anyone to approach: the Grommet Pole.

The Pole was really just an old light pole, set up in the carpark sometime in the 60s to help illuminate the new surf-club building. How did it become the Grommet Pole? No one can recall the exact circumstances. Fatty Al thinks it was just one of those things, a kid surfer being just too cheeky, the older blokes searching for a suitable punishment and tying the young offender to the pole in the meantime.

But whatever it was the Grommet Pole became a great instrument of discipline. Grommets who showed any insolence around the pool table at Surfin' Ern's Beachside Café, or who got in the way in the surf, would be chased down, tied to the Pole with whatever came to hand and left to be rescued hours later by a kindly old lady or an older bloke who took pity.

Fatty Al reckons the main Polekeeper was Witty because he was the fastest runner. "I missed a few of the Pole incidents," swears Witty. "But we had a bunch of little grommets who were cheeky all the time so we had to do something. We used to chase 'em and tie 'em and throw stuff at 'em. Tomatoes and stuff."

Not a grommet escaped in the Pole's greatest years, between 1974 and 1978. The Polemasters were relentless. They had to be – the grommets grew cheekier and faster every year. "They deserved it!" Witty declaims, his voice bulging with righteousness. "They were bloody quick, too, the little bastards . . . They never got hurt, but we scared the hell out of 'em. If I saw people doing it now it wouldn't be so funny. But it was different days then."

Narrabeen surfers came in for their share of flak over the years, mainly because they've won so often. But when Simon Anderson goes out there and turns on with his casual power, there aren't any critics — only admirers.

The Pole's fascination began wearing off around the turn of the decade as the Northy boys grew older, more sensible. By 1982 supergrommet Damien Hardman was able to avoid it altogether. Witty and Anderson took pity on him and took him down to Bells Beach instead, forcing Damien and fellow grommet Greg Anderson to make them cups of tea whenever they felt like it.

You can be serious in the surf only for so long . . .
A Queensland grommet tackles an aerial, forgetting his board on the way.
Inset: Pauline Menzcer gets her kicks with a neat cutback.

Above: Pam Burridge whips a smooth fan of spray off her adopted home break, Newport. Below: When you're young and zany you'll try anything. Did Joel Fitzgerald mean to try this?

TONY NOLAN

The Grommet Pole is still there in the Narrabeen carpark. It hasn't been used for some time. But it's still there, and the legend drifts through the minds of all the grommets at Narrabeen. "Any kid round there knows what it means," says Witty. "You go into the carpark and say: 'Grommet pole!' And they'll run."

But maybe you need better waves than Sydney can provide to pinpoint the very core of this country's surfing soul.

When they picked a short, hot slab of the Gold Coast in Queensland to call "Surfers Paradise," they did the wrong thing. The true surfers' paradise lies some 25 miles (40 kilometers) south of the big buildings and Japanese tourists, just off a twist in the coast next to the Queensland–New South Wales border: the jutting headland of Point Danger, the lovely cove of Rainbow Bay, the long arc of Greenmount; and, framed by two solid rocky groins, the dead-straight wicked strip of sand where a hundred thousand surfers' hopes have lived and died. Kirra.

TONY NOLAN

BURLEIGH HEADS

WAYNE RABBIT BARTHOLOMEW

If Australia is the oldest continent, as is the popular scientific belief, then Mt Warning in far northeastern New South Wales is arguably the most ancient volcano on earth. It hasn't rumbled for 20 million years, so the surrounding land has had all that time to refine and stabilize. The valleys of the Tweed, Currumbin and Tallebudgera undulate gently, punctuated by spurs of granite deposits and rich red-soiled ridges that eventually flow into the sea.

One of these spurs flanks the northern shoulder of Tallebudgera Valley, resolutely meeting the Pacific Ocean in the form of a majestic headland and sitting like a sphinx defiantly turning back the hungry waves.

Burleigh Heads, Queensland, has remained unchanged for millions of years, winning the war between ocean and earth by fortifying its natural base with a terrace of granite boulders. Northward-bound sand flows around the point, anchoring in catchment areas and forming a stabilized sandbank running parallel to the perfectly foiled point. The hollow, powerful waves that wrap serpent-like from the outside cove right through the present-day carpark have only been ridden for 30 years.

Peter Drouyn, Ken Adler and the Neilsen brothers had cut their teeth at Burleigh in the seclusion of the 60s,

occasionally sharing the perfection with nomadic tribesmen Nat Young, Bob McTavish and Gordon Merchant, but it wasn't until the early 70s that the first graphic evidence of hell barrels began to appear in surfing editorials.

My first encounter with big Burleigh was a 1971 inter-club clash pitting the southern Gold Coast, Queensland, trio of Michael Peterson, Peter Townend and myself against Drouyn, Neilsen and co. The Burleigh men hadn't seen Peterson and me, having honed our tube skills at Kirra, a short distance from Burleigh, and it wasn't long before they were watching agape as MP slotted into and out of hideous caves, being literally blown out of impossible sections at breakneck speeds.

The 70s was a vintage decade at

Rabbit knows Burleigh as well as anyone.

Burleigh, highlighted by epic barrels in 73 and 74. The pick of the decade would have to be 75, as Burleigh was saturated by a 28-day swell in April, then bombarded by a series of giant south swells in July. Being pre-leash days it took an extra pump of adrenalin to paddle into a 10-footer (three meters) at the outside cove and drive through sections that could accommodate double-decker buses.

The 1977 Stubbies Classic ushered in the age of pro surfing and after a full week of hectic barrels and perfect conditions, both the MP legend and the Burleigh legend had been enhanced. Surfers from around the world began to make annual pilgrimages to Burleigh to ride the fabled waves.

As another decade unfolds, Burleigh Heads sits sphinx-like, silhouetted against the Pacific backdrop, waiting to become again the centerpiece of Australian surfing as the pro surfing machinery begins warming dormant engines. As the cycle is renewed, Burleigh Heads will undoubtedly showcase the very best surfing on the planet in the best possible waves.

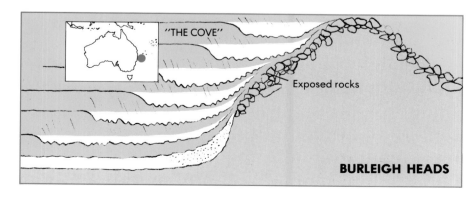

"THE COVE"

Exposed rocks

BURLEIGH HEADS

MARTIN TULLEMANS

104

There's more than a few of those hundred thousand who'd back Kirra Point's claim to be the heart, if not the hub, of Aussie surfing, although some Gold Coasters could spend days discussing the relative merits of Burleigh or Snapper Rocks and never get anywhere.

But they would always come back to Kirra. Coming back to Kirra is something the best Queensland surfers have been doing for over 30 years. In the 1950s, before the arrival of the foam and fiberglass surfboard, the place was almost the sole preserve of the surf clubs. Then, in 1962, Joe Larkin, a former lifeguard from Freshwater in Sydney, headed for the Sunshine State to make surfboards and set up just behind Kirra. By 1965 he had the biggest factory in the state, and the star surfers poured through: Terry Fitzgerald, Peter Townend, Peter Drouyn, George Greenough, even McTavish, who arrived on the back doorstep one day and told Joe's wife: "My name's Bob McTavish and I'm God's gift to surfboard shaping."

By 1970 Kirra was the best-known wave in Australia, a mercilessly fast hollow wall that sucked almost dry on the shallow sandbar next to the point and grew more gruesome as the swell built. Larkin and the boys worked on slicker, sleeker boards to cope with its awesome power, and other manufacturers followed suit. Kirra was one of the few places where surfers like Townend and Wayne "Rabbit" Bartholomew were beginning to ride boards under seven feet (two meters) long inside tubes that were stretching out to 10 or 12 seconds in duration. It was daunting, extreme stuff.

Such a wave demanded a legendary surfer, one whose name would become synonymous with it the way Gerry Lopez's name was synonymous with Hawaii's Banzai Pipeline, or Mickey Dora's was with California's Malibu. And no one was more daunting, more extreme, or in the tube longer than Michael Peterson.

Peterson was an authentic surfing genius who learnt to ride a board at 15 years of age and did it with such terrible grandeur that nobody in Australia or the world could match him. He rode so far inside the Kirra tube that people knew he was there only by the whistling as he warned other surfers off the wave. Between 1972 and 1975 he was literally unbeatable in competition, winning three Bells Beach contests in a row and the inaugural Surfabout, which later developed into one of pro surfing's centerpiece events.

TONY NOLAN

Wayne Bartholomew — Queensland grommet, 1978 world champ, and always way ahead on the international character ratings.

He was god, and when anyone in Australia's cultish 1970s surf community said "MP" you knew whom he or she meant. If Michael did something, anything, it became law. But Michael was shy, and the more he tried to stay out of the limelight, the more it focused him. When he avoided surf contest presentations, the mystique deepened. When rumors of a drug habit spread through the surfing world, the mystique deepened further. When he quit surfing and disappeared underground in 1980, the mystique was impenetrable.

It's hard to say what effect he had on Australian surfing. His disappearing acts hardly made him a contest organizer's best friend. Years later, in a *Tracks* magazine interview, South Africa's Shaun Tomson articulated what more than one pro had thought of Michael: "That guy held surfing back. He held sponsorship back from the sport, he was bad for the sport . . . He was a great surfer, I think he had amazing talent and he was a great surfer. He wasn't good for the sport."

Behind all that, though, there was a whole generation of kids for whom Peterson the rebel meant more than any clean-cut little superstar could ever mean. He was nothing like anyone their parents could approve of, and that was good enough for them.

One of the saddest items of surf-related news popped up in the Sunday papers some time in 1984, when it was announced that MP, traveling under a pseudonym and claiming to be in the employ of the British Secret Service, had been

Sometimes when you've been surfing somewhere like Kirra Point too long, you can just get too casual!

arrested in Brisbane after a manic 17-car cop chase. He subsequently spent some time in a psychiatric institution before being released into his mother's care.

It was a painful tale of a strange era in surfing. But, weird or not, drugs or not, good for the sport or not, nobody has surfed Kirra Point like Peterson.

Maybe Newcastle has Australia's surfing heart in trust at the moment. If you want good surfing, straight and true, it is hard to beat Newcastle.

Newcastle's surfing history stretches deep into the 1920s, when the surf clubs ran the first-ever surfing contests off Newcastle City Beach and the amazing Charles "Snow" McAlister won by doing headstands all the way to the sand.

PETER SIMONS

He never got to ride a thruster, never won $10,000 in a pro contest, but one thing's for sure — no-one loved surfing like Snowy McAlister.

TONY NOLAN

Mark Richards, maybe the greatest surfer of all time, swoops coolly at Dee Why, Sydney.

Newcastle surfers were basically the blokes who didn't turn into bikies. Hilariously rough-and-tumble, they envied the Sydney kids down the road for their exposure to the surf magazines. They had a board-riding club, started by a 60-year-old beach kiosk owner named Vic Thorpe in 1962, and Snow used to come up from his Manly haunts for almost every competition.

There were plenty of good surfers in New-castle as the years rolled on, but no one like Mark Richards. In fact, there was no one in the world like Mark Richards. MR first made his mark by surfing giant Waimea Bay in Hawaii at 17 years of age. Three years later, with the aid of Hawaiian surfboard shaper Reno Abellira, he developed the twin-fin surfboard and used it to win four world pro titles in a row.

Nobody before or since has approached that record. But MR, with his intelligence and easy-going nature, did more than just dominate the competition: he showed the world what the tragic Peterson couldn't – that surfers weren't druggie lunatics, they were normal.

"I think the general impression that people had of surfers in those days was that they were drug addict dole bludgers," MR told a surfing magazine a couple of years after he retired. "I think a lot of it was jealousy. You know, the aver-age guy who drives to work, nine to five, he drives past the beach and there's all these young guys hanging out and going surfing. He's probably jeal-ous that he's not doing it, so the way out is to brand them as degenerates."

MR has a lot to do with the reason why New-castle is indisputably the best producer of hot young riders in Australia today. Look at his godson, for instance. When Mark was first dueling it out

with the great Hawaiians at Waimea Bay, trying to make a name for himself, old-time Novocastrian Robbie Wood was launching his five-year-old son into the Merewether waters.

Now Nicky Wood is one of the world's best surfers, sharing Merewether with a team as brilliant as you'll find on any beach on earth: Luke Egan, Simon Law, Matt Hoy, Dave McArthur and the latest young master, Marcus Brabant.

Newcastle has a big contest now every November, ranking high on the pro tour and a vital stop for world title hopefuls. But the BHP International isn't where the real money is in Australian surfing. That honor is reserved for Torquay.

Torquay is a small town on Victoria's near-west coast, about 70 miles (112 kilometers) from the state capital city of Melbourne. It is small now; 20 years ago it was tiny. But because of the great waves nearby at the fabled Bells Beach and Jan Juc, Torquay was a focus for the Victorian surfing community.

The Torquay crew didn't have surf heroes crawling out of every rockpool like Sydney or the Gold Coast. One great surfer, Wayne Lynch, was born and bred at Lorne, just down the coast, and apart from Wayne and his mate Maurice Cole not

*A*ustralia's two top power surfers, Tom Carroll and Gary Elkerton, really shine when it comes to Hawaii — but they don't mind smashing the odd lip at home, either. **Above**: Tom at Newcastle; **below**: Gary at Bells.

BELLS BEACH

DOUG WARBRICK

PETER SIMONS

The Bells Beach Surfing Recreation Reserve is tucked away on the Victorian coast near the surf town of Torquay. It is an odd-looking place at first sight with crumbling cliffs and brown, coarse sand. When the surf is small you might wonder what all the fuss is about. But when the surf is big, the reason is clear.

Bells is actually two distinct bays, the first being Winkipop Reef, the second being Bells Beach proper where the Rip Curl Pro, the world's longest-running surfing competition, has been held every Easter since 1961. Two special tournament days hold most significance for me.

Easter Sunday, 1965: in the early morning the surf was huge – at least 20 feet (six meters). All the Aussie watermen were there with their 10-feet- 6-inch (three-meter) rhino-chasers, some balsa, some foam with huge stringers, shaped by Pat Curren, Greg Noll or some local ironman.

The wide walls of Bells stand up a long way out, peel down the line and hit the shore break with sometimes heavy consequences. All through its length, there's space for high-performance surfing.
Below: Nicky Wood; right: Mark Occhilupo.

DEAN WILMOT

Only a handful of surfers made it out – locals Peter Troy, Marcus Shaw and Tony Olsen, Russ King and Bob Pike from Sydney, and John Monie from Ocean Beach, New South Wales. John caught the biggest wave ever ridden at Bells, streaking at least 300 yards (273 meters) before pulling out as he reached Winkipop Point, still 100 yards (91 meters) offshore.

By the mid-afternoon rising tide a crowd of several thousand spectators had gathered. Bondi's (Sydney's) Rob Conneeley had already won the grand final on the slack mid-tide and it was time to run the Victorian State titles semifinals. The ocean looked ominous and as the eight local surfers paddled out, the horizon lifted. A 10-wave set broke clear across Bells and Winki more than half a mile (800 meters) to sea.

Who says this only happens in Hawaii? Foam surged over the beach, up the stairs and cliff face and spilled into the carpark! No spectators but plenty of personal items were lost. All the surfers were washed miles down the coast – by

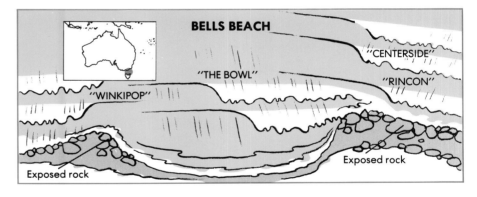

BELLS BEACH

"CENTERSIDE"

"THE BOWL"

"RINCON"

"WINKIPOP"

Exposed rock

Exposed rock

some miracle they all made it in safely – and PA man Olsen declared the State titles abandoned.

Easter Saturday, 1981: early morning, the phone rings. It's "China" Gilbert, the 60-year-old legend and Bells pioneer: "It's booming, the reef must be 20 feet [six meters], it's the best swell since 65!" So, off to Bells. Driving into the carpark I saw Terry Richardson surfing the shore break – it was about 12 feet (3.6 meters). Mark Richards caught a huge wave in the bowl section. It was a solid 15–18 feet (4.5–5.5 meters), but the guys were really only riding from the bowl because no one had real big-wave equipment.

Lots of pros and underground guys rode big waves – MR, Cheyne Horan, Bobby Owens, Richard Cram, Nick Carroll, Derek Hynd; unknown Aussie Gabe Callaghan sealed one of the heats of the day against Nick by riding a set wave entirely across the bay and into Winkipop, disappearing down the line from the judges' view.

A big, fit, young Simon Anderson won the event on a six-foot-six-inch (two-meter) three-fin surfboard, and changed the course of surfing history with the design. The traditional Bells trophies were awarded in the carpark, just the way they are today.

111

Just about all the great Australian surfers have grown up in cities — the Gold Coast, Sydney, Perth. But there's not many of them who'd argue that the best moments in Australian surfing happen way out there, miles from anywhere. Mike McAuliffe carves a beautiful turn on an isolated West Australian wave. **Inset**: Nicky Wood just enjoying a wave at home in Newcastle, New South Wales.

112

PETER SIMONS

Mark Occhilupo — ``Occy'' to
a million grommets worldwide
— is practically as well known
for his flamboyant character as
his incredible surfing. **Above**:
He launches into a perfect
bottom turn at Margaret River.
Right: Even at a contest, he
always has a smile for the
camera.

many Victorian surfers have made an impact on the sport. But what Torquay lacked in numbers it made up for in energy. A couple of keen Bells surfers, Doug Warbrick and Brian Singer, got tired of wearing old football jumpers and thick diving suits in the freezing water and set up a shop where they made surfboards and a new kind of flexible surfing wetsuit for their mates. Fifteen years later, with their company Rip Curl turning over tens of millions, Doug and Brian won Australian design awards and had their favorite surf spot turned into a surfing reserve by an eager-to-please council. Surf clothing label Quiksilver, run by a cunning-minded Alan Green and former Victorian surf champ John Law, followed a similar booming path.

Pretty soon the crew were running a big network of influence throughout Aussie surfing. Grommets from Narrabeen to Perth wore their gear. They sponsored events and hot young surfers all over the place. Their big contest, the Bells Easter event, was an absolute necessity for traveling pros. But their biggest moves came in the early 80s, when licensees for both major Torquay companies began operating in America, Japan and Europe.

It was groundbreaking stuff. You could count on one hand the number of Australian industries that have established themselves internationally;

and one finger of the hand would be surfing. As much as any pro surfer, the Torquay Mafia carried something of Australia's heart and soul into the world.

So. Is it Kirra? Narrabeen? Bells? Newcastle Beach? McTavish's Byron home? Maybe. Maybe a mix of all five. But I like to think the heart of Australian surfing is a long, long way from all these places, somewhere off the desert north of Geraldton, Western Australia, where at this very moment Captain and the Hawk may well be cracking waves of dimensions that'd make your eyes pop.

Nobody has ever heard of these two but they're keen enough surfers to make any world champ look bored. The Hawk is a short, stocky, fiery bloke, a quick talker with piercing blue eyes who gets himself hired out from the Fremantle docks as a boat captain for the rich and clumsy.

Captain has a crayfish boat that he runs off the mid-west coast. He is tall, quiet as the Hawk is noisy, and his eyes are slits from the sun. Between them they've been surfing about 25 years.

When they come back out of the desert for a bit of work or civilization, they like to talk about their surf spot: just one quarter-mile (400-meter) reef in the remotest stretch of all that 15,000 surfable miles of Australian coast.

"D'yer reckon it's as good as Bali?" Captain will ask, squinting and looking down one side of his nose. And the Hawk will wave his arms and grunt with Australian certainty, and say it's better than Bali, better than anything those Yanks surf, better than what he used to surf back in Queensland when he was a kid, probably better than what they ride in Hawaii, even.

"After all, mate," he'll say, while Captain nods solemnly in agreement, "home's where the heart is. Right?"

MARGARET RIVER

TOM CARROLL

For me, Margaret River is a very special place.

Margaret sits along the southwest edge of Western Australia, right in the teeth of some of the most fearsome oceanic elements provided by the planet – the Roaring Forties. These fierce gales, blowing for thousands of miles across the Indian Ocean, whip up huge swells that run straight into the limestone cliffs and reefs of the southwest.

About halfway along the southwest coastal strip the Margaret River winds peacefully through its small valley down to the ocean, where just to the south one of those limestone reefs produces a big breaking left-hand wave with an imposing face and enough strength to do plenty of damage.

It was first surfed by a schoolteacher named Warren McKinney and a mate in the early 1960s. They dodged the blackboy trees along the gravel track from the Margaret township six miles (9.5 kilometers) inland and surfed the

river secretly for several years, while most West Aussie surfers stayed at Yallingup some distance north. In the mid-1960s, Margaret was regularly surfed by riders such as Murray Smith, Lindsay Thompson and later Robert Conneeley.

In 1968 Margaret caught some of the world's best surfers totally off-guard at the Australian Titles, producing clean 10-foot (three-meter) surf during the entire week of the competition. Since that week, Margaret has been one of the world's favorite spots for competitive and hard-core surfing.

In 1978 I was 16 years old, surfing as a junior in the National Titles at Margaret, when I was confronted with the biggest surf I'd ever seen – for my first heat! All I had was a six-foot (1.8-meter) board and about 108 pounds (49 kilograms) of flesh to tackle ocean swells of 10–12 feet (3–3.5 meters). I remember having to float weightlessly, eyes closed and bowels loose, down my

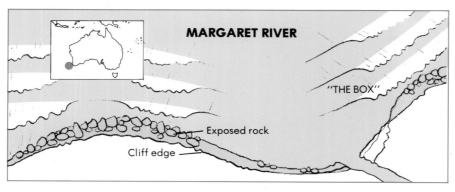

MARGARET RIVER

"THE BOX"

Exposed rock

Cliff edge

BRIAN HUGHES

Good Margaret does one thing very well — it gives you room to move, and heaps of it. **Left**: *Dave Davidson gets every inch of rail into his turn.* **Above**: *Tom Carroll, undisputed master of the River.*

first few waves, not quite understanding that I was in the process of being broken into big-wave riding. The initial sense of fear was overcome by the sheer thrill of surfing way out in the middle of the ocean, as the spray off the massive waves blinded my view of the shoreline. As I came in from that heat the thought of winning was only a secondary consideration. I was overwhelmed by the power that I had been so close to, and from which I had escaped.

From that trip until my next, in 1987, I constantly thought about the wave and how I would approach it. I knew I would have to go back there some day.

At last, nine years later, a major professional contest was scheduled for

the river and I knew this was my opportunity to surf Margaret the way I'd wanted to for so long. From my first surf all the way to the final of the contest, Margaret River's thick walls seemed to cradle the sleek narrow boards I'd worked on with shapers Phil Byrne and Pat Rawson. I felt the confidence of almost a decade's surfing in Hawaii, where even bigger waves roar through on the reefs of Pipeline and Sunset Beach. From grommet to professional: this was one of the best moments of my surfing life.

New Zealand and the South Pacific

A SURFING DREAM

TERRY FITZGERALD

Three waves of Asian migration have spread through the Pacific Basin over the last millennium. The last created a form of celestial open ocean navigation. It was this third wave of seafarers that populated the far reaches of the Pacific and mastered the art of riding waves.

While first the Melanesians and then the Micronesians used raft and canoe to island-hop their cultures through the western island chains, it was the Polynesians who took their ocean-going canoes to the extremities of the world's largest body of water. Perhaps it was in these canoes that the Polynesians discovered the art of riding the ocean.

Visualize a long, clean, ground swell rising from the Great Southern Ocean's Roaring Forties and sweeping through the mid-Pacific Islands. The very nature of the intrepid ocean-going Polynesians has their tapa sails set with the trailing southeast trade wind and the canoe crew paddling in unison, discovering the thrill of careering along on nature's most enigmatic phenomenon.

Climatically the islands of the South Pacific vary radically. From those that take the full brunt of the Antarctic's cold fronts, like the South Island of New Zealand, the Chathams and Easter Island, to the balmy isles of the Marquesas and the

There's nowhere in the world where the water is bluer, the sun is brighter or the waves better than Tahiti. Here Vetea David throws himself off the lip at Ha'piti, Moorea.

PETER SIMONS

Samoas, sweltering in the tropical doldrums. The calm is periodically broken by hurricane and cyclone, but there is always one all-encompassing factor to influence life throughout the Basin – the sea and its spoils.

Surfing New Zealand is a race against time. The islands sit in the path of the seven low-pressure cells that continually march their way around the bottom of the world. As these lows slingshot off the bottom of Australia they bring swells, with wind and rain, to the west coast of New Zealand – a one-, two- or three-day cycle that has surfers anticipating the onslaught and the aftermath of the continual flow of cold fronts. Scampering from the west to the east and back again becomes almost obligatory.

The classic New Zealand surf spot is three-pointed Raglan Bay. Sitting in the path of southerly and westerly swells, it's a rare day when there isn't surf. Conditions can vary, of course, but the power and size of Indicators and the lineup of Whale Bay are equal to anywhere in the world.

To the far north is another classic left; at the base of Ninety Mile Beach the western reaches of Wreck Bay provide numerous points for mile after mile of lefts to peel through. For the inside bays and reefs to work the swell has to be huge, and for

PETER SIMONS

North Island, New Zealand, is right in the middle of some important trade routes. It's also right in the middle of some major swell patterns. **Above**: Sponge Bay captures some of that swell and turns it into a nice lefthander. **Right**: An interesting place to be.

that to happen the southerly wind bringing the waves will also bring in the dirty weather from the obliging Tasman Sea.

The east coast of the North Island relies on northerly swells from subtropical lows in the Coral Sea for its best surf. The Coramondel Peninsula and The Mount can turn on, but it's Great Barrier Island in the Hauraki Gulf that provides the archetypal New Zealand surf spot. Rolling hills, idyllic beaches and a mixture of rivermouth, beach and point breaks that take the edge off the rawness of the west coast.

That edge comes back with a vengeance on the southeastern and southern coasts. The Gisborne Pipeline and the Mahia Peninsula's Rolling Stone reef provide the punch in the vicinity of Captain Cook's first landfall on the islands of the Long White Cloud.

Cook provides a thread throughout the Pacific Islands, and it was he who first recorded Hawaiian royalty's propensity for surfing. But it is the islands of these kings' forefathers that hold a plethora of reefs reeling off barrel after barrel.

The French Polynesian islands don't have the same mix as Hawaiian surf. Hawaii's volcanic origins have eroded to become a perfect combination of beach and reef. Polynesia doesn't have this bal-

ance. The living coral and offshore reefs of the South Pacific provide another kind of perfection. With open-ocean swell speed a knot faster, the surge of that swell out of the depths turns waves square as they freight-train hundreds of feet in unrideable majesty. That closeout can become surfable as the swell turns and with a few degrees of difference, the lip line opens up and turns into tube time.

Open-ocean spots such as Ha'piti become awesome as waves that are nearly seven feet (two meters) high become the same distance wide as they hit the reef. On the other side of Moorea,

Hawaiians love heading south to experience the waves of other islands. Here Todd Chesser carves back down the face in Fiji.

JEFF HORNBAKER

TAVARUA

RICHARD CRAM

DON KING

"Sorry you can't surf here . . . this is private property!'' exclaimed the large Fijian as he wheeled his boat in the direction of a suitable anchoring spot. His passengers, all guests at Tavarua island surf camp, have sole right to surf the incredible waves of Cloud Break surf. By law.

Cloud Break is the name given to a coral reef situated roughly five miles (eight kilometers) off the main island of Fiji. More or less in the middle of nowhere, the reef and the waves that break along it are private. The right to surf these waves is held exclusively by

JEFF HORNBAKER

the owners of the surf camp, and these rights are vigilantly guarded. Understandably so, their business depends on it.

Tavarua, the world's premier surf camp, is but a leisurely afternoon's travel north-northeast of Sydney.

To spend time on Tavarua is not so much a surfing adventure in the spirit of exploring uncharted coastline with only one other companion. It's more a recreational retreat where your choice of sport is surfing, fishing, skindiving, or hammock slouching. All at US$100 a day.

The principal allure of Tavarua for the surfer is access to the incredible waves of Cloud Break and Tavarua reef. Cloud Break is a fast-breaking lefthander that winds along a live coral reef. It is very much like Uluwatu in Indonesia in that it can take on many different moods, depending on swell and tide. Add the consistent calm of the tropics and you have, quite simply, one of the best waves in the world.

However, the very best wave in the area is found on the reef that hugs Tavarua island – right in front of the restaurant. This wave breaks in a more perfect pattern than that of Cloud Break and its special feature is that it grows in size and intensity as the surfer rides along. Definitely no cutbacks, just full speed ahead.

Tavarua, the commercial enterprise, is designed with the professional surfer in mind, catering to the needs of American surfing businessmen.

The bungalows, though sparsely furnished, are comfortable. There's no air-conditioning, television, radio or electronic entertainment. Reading and conversation make up the main evening pastimes. Hot showers are via five-gallon (22-liter) solar water bags. The meals range from okay to excellent, depending on how the fishing is going. Breakfast is substantial, lunch is usually sandwiches and fruit and the evening meal usually fish.

In the 1970s, to experience the ideal surfing lifestyle one really had to get off life's train, so as to be allowed the time to explore for perfect uncrowded waves. In the late 80s, and more frequently in the 90s, surf camps such as Tavarua will allow working surfers the opportunity of enjoying all the very best that surfing has to offer. Without the necessity of having to use large chunks of time in order to surf perfect, uncrowded waves. Allowing the ideal surfing lifestyle to be more like: "HOLD THE TRAIN . . . I'LL BE BACK IN TEN!"

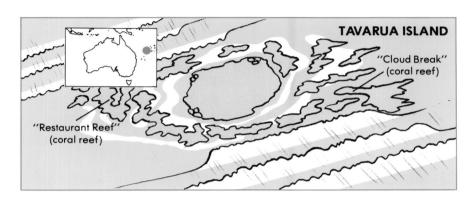

TAVARUA ISLAND

"Cloud Break" (coral reef)

"Restaurant Reef" (coral reef)

The spot most surfers dream about at Tavarua is Cloud Break, a wonderful reef setup some half a mile (800 meters) offshore. Here waves wrap around coral with all the grace you'd expect of a tropical paradise. **Far left**: *Which board?* **Spread**: *Tom Carroll just takes a peek out from behind the curtain before going back in for an extended stay.*

123

In a world where dirty water drives surfers crazy and you sometimes can't even get a wave for fear of running someone over, it's nice to know that there are places where true purity — in surfing and sea water — still exists. **Spread**: Tom Carroll's perfect bottom turn. **Inset**: Simon Law relishes the lagoon's peace.

JEFF HORNBAKER

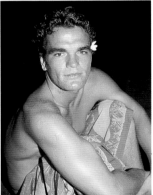

JEFr HORNBAKER

Above and right: **V**etea David
is Tahiti's surfing ambassador to
the world, coming out of his
dreamlike hideaway to win a
world junior championship and
go on to professional success.
Despite the fame and glory, he
loves to go home — who
wouldn't? **Below**: *Another*
perfect reef.

JEFF HORNBAKER

Temae sits and waits for the due south swell that is big enough to squeeze by Tahiti-Nui and peel perfectly down what is arguably one of the most dangerous inside coral beaches in the world. Temae works through few winter swells, but there is the occasional day when the wind and swell direction is right and Temae does a fair imitation of Jeffreys Bay, as waves wheel back into the reef and wind off.

The main island of Tahiti is not endowed with any perfect spots. However, there is so much reef and so much surf that with a car and/or a boat (which is a committed surfer's necessity), a burn around the island will turn up rideable waves no matter what the wind or swell condition.

From the eastern shore black-sand beaches to the outside reefs off Maara, Tahiti covers the full spectrum of a surfer's paradise. Ta'apuna, the closest reef-pass combo to Papeete (much like Ala Moana is to Honolulu – without the marina), typifies the Tahitian surf spot.

JEFF HORNBAKER

A late drop and you're looking through crystal-clear water at a coral bottom mottled with the fingers of deeper depths and thoughts of razor cuts. Hitting the flat provides the power point to punch under the lip which appears to be reaching for your head in a cacophony of roars that deepen the tighter you tuck. Peel off and pull in, blasting for the open door. Only when the bowl swings back, threatening to shut down, does the thought of being bombed, pitched and face-planted on coral force a move through the back to peel your eyelids back at the approaching surges of a 10-wave set with your heartbeat bordering on tattoo.

Adrenalin: yes! Performance: how balls-up are you?

Polynesia works mostly on south to southwest swells. Outer-island spots like Miri Miri on Raiatea are genuine big-wave line drives. There are others that take the last gasps of north swells that have battered Hawaii. The perfection of a swell that has negotiated the equatorial zones to reach Huahine

A smart man, Rob Bain, wears a helmet just in case a thick Cloud Break lip picks him off and takes him for a little trip down to the coral.

leaves nothing to the imagination. Fabulous Fare gauche and Fare droit line the pass to Fare harbor. At the other end of the lagoon, at Fiti, the same reef out-Velzys Velzyland.

Throughout the islands are mixes of atolls and reefs. The exploration of the Pacific was initiated by the third-wave Polynesians. The fourth wave, following in the wake of islander canoes, are surfers.

The Cook Islands, Samoas, Fiji and New Caledonia are already being surfed on a regular basis. The Isles de Gambier are an outpost beckoning . . . How many other spots are there in the vastness of the Pacific Ocean?

Enough for my lifetime!

AARON CHANG

Hawaii
THE TESTING GROUND

MICHAEL LATRONIC

Surfing in Hawaii. You can't touch it. Hawaiian wave riding enjoys an ambience like no other surfing culture. From whatever nook or cranny your surfing world hails, wherever in the world you've learned to surf or have heard of surfing, "the sport of Hawaiian kings" is the genesis and core of what we surfers claim as our lifestyle. Indeed, earlier civilizations than the Hawaiians, in South America and Polynesia, had ridden swells on crude canoe-like vessels, but it was only in Hawaiian history that riding waves on boards became a cultural pastime.

Historically, as with many other island and coastal societies, the Hawaiians were attuned to the ocean through necessity. They relied on it for both food and transportation. Since Hawaiians kept no formal written history, the exact details of when the sport was born will probably never be known. Ancient chants passed down from generation to generation tell us that surfing was a loved and cherished amusement as well as a competitive sport long before the beginning of the fifteenth century. Surfing was practised on every island by both men and women but there were designated spots and surfboard designs reserved for royalty and commoners, the longboards and the big waves being reserved for the higher classes.

The first Westerner to see surfing was the famous Captain James Cook in the 1770s at Kealakekua Bay on the Big Island of Hawaii. The astounded sea captain described the sight eloquently:

"The surf, which breaks on the coast around the bay, extends to the distance of about 150 yards

Surfing in Hawaii is all about big walls, big boards and big hearts. Mark Foo knows the meaning of all three, especially at Waimea Bay.

DEAN WILMOT

Matt Kechele slams his board through a move he might well do at home in Florida — except at Rocky Point it happens twice as fast.

from the shore, within which space the surges of the sea, accumulating from the shallowness of the water, are dashed against the beach with prodigious violence. Whenever, from stormy weather or any extraordinary swell at sea, the impetuosity of the surf is increased to its utmost height, they choose this time for amusement . . .''

By the early 1800s Western missionaries nipped all that fun-loving, aloha-spirit-in-the-surf right in the bud. Surfing all but vanished, condemned as a frivolous and distracting activity in the face of almighty, ''holy'' pursuits. The nudity and party-like antics were uncomplementary. Perhaps this is where surfers got their lazy, good-for-nothing attributes and reputation . . . ! At the turn of the century, as the missionary influence ebbed, many inhabitants of the Waikiki area were surfing regularly. In 1908 the Outrigger Canoe Club and Hui Nalu (Club of the Waves) was formed, ''to give an added and permanent attraction to Hawaii and to make Waikiki always the home of the surfer.'' George Freeth and Duke Kahanamoku were the most notable early patrons of the sport and traveled abroad popularizing it worldwide.

Now look at what they've done! Not a single day goes by without a tremble or a spasm from this absolute addiction we've grown to know and love, and Hawaii is where it all started. The sport became a cult both on mainland America and in Australia, but "the islands" were still the place to go for the ultimate surf trek. Through the roaring 20s and in and out of the two world wars, surfing marched on in Hawaii, which became, through prestige, trial and experience, the surfing world's most important arena.

Without refute, Hawaii claims the most challenging and radical surf in the world. Much of this is due to the huge swells produced annually in the Aleutian area and the shapely yet dangerous coral reefs which surround the island from the depths of the Pacific. Sans a continental shelf to disperse the ocean's energy, swells generated by huge low-pressure systems in the far north of the Pacific thunder on the Hawaiian coastline more fiercely than any other place on the planet. Consequently, Hawaiian surfing nurtures absolute clout, ultimate danger – and ultimate rewards. It's a thrill-seekers' dream; a paradox balancing pleasure, beauty, pain and horror.

Tom Carroll caught in one of those Sunset Beach moments only the very innovative or the plain crazy get into.

SUNSET BEACH

ROD KIRSOP

Sunset Beach is the most challenging wave in the world. Waimea Bay may have the biggest waves, Pipeline the hollowest, Kirra and Jeffreys and Grajagan the most perfect, but Sunset is the most demanding. It is the ultimate test of a surfer's ability.

From the beach it can appear deceptively easy. Big peaks rising slowly, breaking far out to sea, before rolling gracefully into a tubular inside section. Deep-blue water, clear skies, the tradewinds rustling the palm fronds completes this idyllic tropical scene. Even the paddle out in the deep channel looks a simple matter.

But once in the water, the true power and immensity of the break becomes apparent. The channel is a raging torrent, capable of sweeping unwary swimmers and lost surfboards a mile or more out to sea in a matter of minutes. The big peaks, which from the beach seemed to break so gracefully, are raw ocean swells that have not been slowed by any continental shelf, nor subdued by any offshore reefs. They are huge violent masses of water which rise up suddenly and break with ferocious intent.

The lineup is difficult, at times impossible to predict. There is the north peak, the northwest peak and the mighty west peak. When the swell is from a single direction a surfer can reasonably predict where the next set will peak, but every so often a maverick wave will sweep through, catching many surfers inside, forcing them to abandon their boards and dive deep beneath the tumultuous masses of whitewater. On many days, however, there is a combination of swell directions, and the takeoff zone lies anywhere within an area the size of three to four football fields. Getting caught inside can become a regular occurrence. The ability of

MARTIN TULLEMANS

JOLI

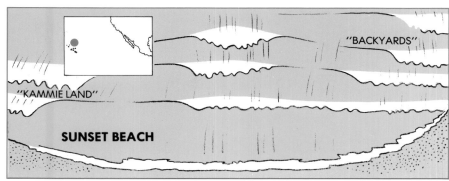

"BACKYARDS"

"KAMMIE LAND"

SUNSET BEACH

surfers to position themselves correctly for takeoff is a combination of skill, knowledge, experience, patience, intuition, and luck. There are few who have mastered the Sunset Beach lineup.

The next challenge is the drop. The stiff tradewinds hold up the lip of the breaking wave till the very last moment, the spray blowing back in a huge white plume, the wave becoming steeper and steeper. The surfer strokes hard into the blinding wind and spray, feels the board being lifted up as the peak rises ever higher. Swiftly he leaps to his feet and takes the sheer mad hell-long drop, the wind and water rushing up the face of the wave, the spray in his eyes, the board almost airborne. Recovering his balance at the bottom of the wave, his board chattering across the water at maximum speed, he begins his turn, sinking as much of the surfboard's rail into the water as he can to turn around the mountain of whitewater bearing down on him.

What the wave does next is a matter of variables. Depending on the swell size and direction, the tide, the strength of the tradewinds and the waves in the preceding set, the wave may fill up and back off, or stand up and close out, or it may fire down the line in a perfect hollow wall, allowing the best surfers to maneuver their boards into radical positions, carving top turns and snapbacks. Most ordinary surfers struggle to hold a trim line tight enough to beat the racing curl.

At the end of the wave is the inside section. A seething, sucking, smoking tube, it produces some of the deepest, biggest and most amazing tube rides ever witnessed.

To surf Sunset is to experience the ultimate in surfing. The size, the power and the speed of the waves are on a completely different scale from anywhere else. They are rarely perfect, but their faults make them all the more challenging. And the insane rush of riding a wave from the peak to the inside bowl is everything that surfing can offer.

You know Sunset as soon as you look at it: big, thick, windy and asking all the skills a surfer has — even from the best.
Top: *Gary Elkerton.* **Bottom**: *Tom Curren.*

PETER SIMONS

To this day, Hawaii still enjoys a large share of the limelight in progressive surfing although with the imminent commercialization of the sport, some attention has been diverted to smaller waves elsewhere. In the early stages of surfing, however, Hawaii was always considered the Mecca. No surfer was complete without having touched Hawaiian saltwater.

It is this belief that gives Hawaiian surfing its ambience, every bit as much as its rich history. The only way I can think of quantifying this is to draw analogies: Hawaiian surfing is the Wimbledon of tennis, the Detroit of auto-making or the Tokyo of electronic gadgetry. Many of the early professional events were centered in Hawaii and as the sport grew sufficiently to have its own circuit, Hawaiian waters enjoyed most of the points and money; certainly all the glory. And it was the surfers in Hawaii who were the pioneers in performance surfing, especially in big waves. Contests or not, whether they flew in from Australia or California or were born and raised in the islands, legends like Buzzy Trent, Terry Fitzgerald, Nat Young, Barry Kanaiapuni, Eddie Aikau, Gerry Lopez, Reno Abellira, Owl Chapman, Sam Hawk, Ben Aipa,

AARON CHANG

DEAN WILMOT

Hawaii is not all hair-raising big waves — it's moments of grace and timing on small ones too. **Left:** Pam Burridge launches off Rocky Point. **Above:** John Shortis slices a lovely foamy face at Off-the-Wall.

David Nuuhiwa, and Jeff Hakman all made their mark in Hawaiian surf. BK, Reno, Hawk and Chapman all took to the field on self-made equipment, BK and Reno tending the Hawaiian roots design forum and the latter hailing from the Dick Brewer school. All these guys did serious work in carving big reputations in big surf. Although Brewer himself never emerged as a fantastic surfer, his designs in the 1970s considerably advanced the style of wave riding.

Hawaiian surfers for the most part developed their styles around the tremendous power with which they dealt in the surf. Hawaiian surfing is strong and unguided. The waves dictate the ride.

In each surfing generation, there's one or two surfers whose whole style and approach to wave riding fits Hawaiian power perfectly. When this happens, it doesn't matter how they do in small surf, or how good they are at public speaking, or how many mates they have. Simply, their names become legend: Gary Elkerton.

THE BANZAI PIPELINE

BARTON LYNCH

After ten years of traveling and surfing some of the best waves on the planet, I have never come across a wave that stirs my emotions like the Banzai Pipeline. It scares me, truly scares me and at the same time it challenges and thrills me like nothing else. The Pipeline is located between Sunset Beach and Waimea Bay on the north shore of the Hawaiian island of Oahu.

During the months October through March huge swells batter the shallow lava reef – and most daredevil surfers who challenge it. It is without doubt the

The sheer ruthless power of Pipeline, with someone helpless in its jaws, is hard to comprehend. Todd Holland and his board get ready for a trip to hell.

world's most dangerous wave.

The Pipeline got its name from the perfect cylindrical tubes that break a mere 160 feet (50 meters) from the shoreline, making it one of the best spectator waves. Sitting on the beach you can feel the sand tremble beneath you as waves explode.

Those perfect Pipeline tubes don't happen every day, they are a rare gem in the surfing experience. Your best chances, though, are later in the season as sand builds up on the reef during the flat summer months and warps the shape of the wave, at times making it unrideable. It is not until a few big swells roll through that the sand is washed away and the reef is returned to its true shape. West swells up to 15 feet (4.5 meters) are best, and an easterly wind offshore.

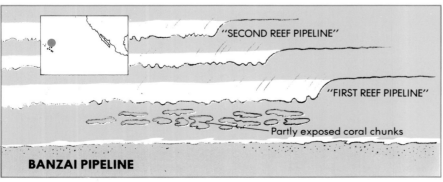

"SECOND REEF PIPELINE"

"FIRST REEF PIPELINE"

Partly exposed coral chunks

BANZAI PIPELINE

*T*hree good angles at the Pipe — Gerry Lopez's masterful surfing above water, the coral and lava waiting below, and what happens when you don't quite manage the former and come in contact with the latter.

The Pipeline has been the site of some of surfing's most tragic and triumphant moments. In 1981 tragedy struck the Pipeline Masters. Two expert big-wave riders, Florida's Steve Massefeller and Californian Chris Lundy, both came to grief, victims of the Pipeline. Massefeller wiped out while attempting a late takeoff. The wave dumped him head-first into the reef, he was knocked unconscious and rescued only when his board surfaced and water patrollers could follow his legrope from the board to him. He was revived on the beach and taken to hospital where he underwent major skull surgery and spent a long time in intensive care. Steve was very lucky

lost. The legendary Pipeline master Gerry Lopez once said that it was not a matter of *whether* you were going to get hurt at the Pipeline but more a matter of *when*.

On the brighter side, the images of past Pipeline legends will last forever – from Phil Edwards, the first person ever to surf there, through to Lopez and Rory Russell on to Shaun Tomson, Mark Richards, Dane Kealoha and Mike Ho.

There is a new guard today, people like Derek Ho, Ronnie Burns, John Gomes and Tom Carroll to name just a few. Some of the victories there have been spectacular, like Mike Ho's in 82 with a broken wrist in a cast, and his younger brother Derek's perfect 10-point

AARON CHANG

TED GRAMBEAU

and today is working as a lifeguard in Florida.

In the very next heat Lundy also wiped out and was driven onto the reef knees first. He needed total reconstruction of one knee and today surfs with a huge brace.

Injuries are a common occurrence at the Pipeline and some lives have been

tube ride to win in 86. My greatest moment came at the Pipeline on January 2, 1989 when I won the Billabong Pro and the world title. A day that I will cherish forever.

For thrill, excitement and challenge the Pipeline is without comparison. Once ridden successfully, it makes most other waves fade into insignificance.

ROB GILLEY

The speed and acceleration which characterize mid-Pacific surf allow the surfer to draw lines and carve freely. There is no pumping or groveling for momentum. Conversely, Hawaiian surfing breeds control and flow. The resulting style is a pleasure to watch.

If there was just one person to name from the 70s who overwhelmed the world with lengthy and graceful tube tactics, it would be Gerry Lopez, the undisputed lifetime achiever at the infamous Banzai Pipeline. Through his zen-like performances and the gift of modern celluloid, the surfing world would grasp what being one with nature is all about.

The Hawaiian mystique grew even more as surf flicks like *Five Summer Stories* and *Free Ride*, depicting the awesome Hawaiian waves, filled movie houses. Nowadays, at peak season, not a single good day goes by unfilmed, -videoed or -recorded for the world to witness. Hawaii has proven itself to be by far the most colorful and dramatic place of action water photography. On good surf days, one can hardly count the lenses.

But of course it hasn't been the saleability of Hawaiian surfing that has brought it to a pinnacle, it is more the reality of it. Surfing Hawaii mid-season is and always will be a gut-wrenching, death-defying experience; the world knows it. The most electrifying surfing events in Hawaii have

been such classics as the Duke, the Smirnoff, the Pipeline Masters and more recently the Billabong Pro and Eddie Aikau Memorial.

For a short period the Hawaii hype dwindled. Its importance, however, was not forgotten. Towards the end of the 1970s and into the 80s, something happened. While guys like Dane Kealoha, Mike Ho, Buttons Kaluhiokalani, Larry Bertlemann, Buzzy Kerbox and Hans Hedemann enjoyed good results on the International Pro Surfing tour, the tour itself underwent a strange and temporary change of direction.

Since the inception of a world pro tour, Hawaii had enjoyed top billing as the grand finale of the world championship year. This had a lot to do with the fact that Fred Hemmings, organizer and owner of pro surfing's ruling body, the IPS (International Professional Surfing), also happened to be the owner and promoter of the Hawaiian contests. But in most people's minds it also had a lot to do with the even plainer fact that Hawaii was where surfers were **surfers**, and no mistake.

But many surfers were unhappy with the Hemmings approach, especially his lack of willingness to go all out in pulling a world tour together, rather

Over the years Martin Potter's been everywhere on Hawaiian waves — sometimes to places he might rather have avoided. **Left**: *At Backdoor;* **below**: *at Sunset;* **bottom**: *at Off-the-Wall.*

TED GRAMBEAU

than allow events to run willy-nilly worldwide. When top surfer Ian Cairns formed his own organization, the Association of Professional Surfers (ASP), the tour pros found themselves demanding things of Fred that Fred wasn't prepared to give. Like sanction fees. And rules the same as other contests. Suddenly the Hawaiian tour was off the ratings. The best Hawaiians, like Mike Ho and Dane Kealoha, were being fined for taking part in their hometown events.

Bad as it was for the Hawaiians, for pro surfing itself this was near-tragedy. Hawaii's huge surf was potentially its biggest drawcard. Not only that – surfers all over the planet were asking the same thing: "Can you have a world champ who doesn't surf Hawaii?" Nobody liked it, not even Cairns, whose reputation was made in big Hawaiian waves. When the tour finally returned to Hawaii for a big event in 1985 with the Billabong Pro, the whole surfing world breathed a sigh of relief. Now Hawaii is again where the title is decided, and most touring pros agree that while competing hard in small waves around the world has its merit, absolute mettle and talent must be tested in Hawaii's liquid proving ground.

Over the years Hawaiian surfers have set themselves apart from the rest of the world. Take, for instance, Dane Kealoha and watch his magnificent charge on any day at backdoor Pipeline; aggression and instinct combine into a pinnacle of

141

DEAN WILMOT

PETER BROUILLET

Above: **S**haun Tomson carves confidently at Rocky Point.
Below: Eddie Aikau's memorial and, **opposite**, the vast expanse
he once called home — Waimea Bay.

talent, sort of inbred. He epitomizes the Hawaiian style. He makes it appear to be second nature to him – so much so that the subtleties evade the untrained eye. In his heyday Kealoha found himself runner-up on the world tour ratings and the most feared competitive force from Hawaii. To this day, Dane's act in Hawaii is hard to beat and that qualifies him as one of the best in the world.

On one legendary day in 1967, the wild-haired Eddie Aikau once paddled straight through the landed "haole" pack at Waimea Bay and proceeded to pick off the biggest, baddest 25-foot (7.5-meter) waves. He took off further over on the inside of the peak than anyone and to this day that zone is known as "Eddie's Bowl." His peers tell us that Eddie used to grin and chuckle while on these rides. Having lost his life at sea in 1978 in a rescue attempt, the Hawaiian soul of Eddie Aikau lives on with every person riding Hawaiian waves for pure joy.

And look at the surfing of another big-wave waterman, Darrick Doerner. Here's a guy who takes off behind the peak at 12–15 foot

WAIMEA BAY

MARK FOO

Waimea Bay, sitting right in the middle of Hawaii's awesome North Shore stretch of coast, is generally considered to be the biggest rideable wave in the world. It is also home to that even more frightening surfing concept – the Unridden Realm.

Almost all the rules in surfing over the past three decades have been bent or broken. The terms "impossible" and "unrideable" have been redefined again and again. The boundaries of performance are being pushed back every day. Generations of champions, heroes and "wannabees" have come and gone. But for more than 30 years now, the only line that hasn't been redrawn, or even crossed, is that of the biggest wave ever ridden.

Waimea is only a small bay, maybe half a mile (800 meters) across. It's amazing how much oceanic energy it can soak up. While other North Shore spots like Sunset Beach are wild cauldrons of foam, the Bay is just beginning to break properly. The true Waimea takeoff spot comes into being in swells of around 18 feet (5.5 meters), and really opens up over 20 feet (six meters). The 25-foot (7.6-meter) days are reserved for the best of the Waimea regulars. And over 30 feet (nine meters) – that's where the Unridden Realm comes into play.

Make no mistake, there have been some monstrous waves surfed at the Bay. There are quite a few people who've

ridden waves with good control just this side of the line. In 1988 I saw Darrick Doerner take the biggest wave I've ever seen ridden. In 1990 I watched Brock Little tread a fine line on a wave that broke clean across the Bay. Mark Richards rode a couple of mackers in the 1986 Billabong contest. Certainly Ken Bradshaw has been right out to the border a few times, and according to James Jones, Rodger Erickson had "a really big one" in 1981.

Yet no one can claim to have ridden waves bigger than did the great pioneers of big-wave Waimea surfing – Ricky Grigg, Peter Cole, Buzzy Trent, Greg Noll, Pat Curren, George Downing, Jose Angel and Eddie Aikau.

There have been attempts – not many, since waves of the Unridden variety are few enough, and people with the guts, ability and desire to try clawing into them are even fewer. But while each attempt has brought us closer to a successful ride on a wave over 30 feet, the result is always the same – disaster.

On November 28, Thanksgiving Day, 1974, a 22-year-old James Jones caught a wave that was at least five feet (1.5 meters) bigger than anything else that came through on that 25-foot-plus

day. The result was a spinal subluxation and a lifesaving rescue by Eddie Aikau. Ricky Grigg says his biggest wave was back in 1982, and thinks it was board failure a third of the way down that wiped him out – the price, a fractured neck and three months in traction.

Perhaps it is just a question of a faster board, one that will overcome the sheer physical problem of making it down the wave face. Perhaps it is a matter of being in the right place at the right time, in the right frame of mind. But the fact is that Waimea's biggest surf remains unridden – and that's as good a reason as any to get us out there.

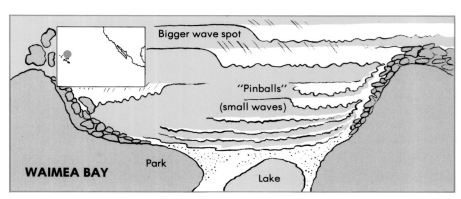

Bigger wave spot

"Pinballs" (small waves)

WAIMEA BAY   Park

Lake

The critical moment at the Bay comes right at the takeoff. **Top**: Glen Winton in the middle of a lot of water. **Left**: Richard Schmidt, stylish in a terrifying situation. **Above**: If these two guys didn't admit to each other that they were just a bit scared, they lied.

146

It doesn't matter where this man surfs, he can still slam that lip. Tom Curren shows his classic form at Off-the-Wall. **Inset**: Marvin Foster hangs coolly back inside a lime-green barrel at Third Dip.

(3.6–4.5 meter) Sunset with no fear. His bravado at Waimea is equally a quirk of nature. In November of 1989, Doerner paddles out into 25–30 foot (7.5–9 meter) surf at 7 a.m. to deliver leis at "Eddie's Bowl." Aside from proving to be a brother of Hawaiian surfing, Darrick is considered to be the greatest underground big-wave rider in the world.

Then there's Johnny Gomes, who finds small-wave riding to his disadvantage yet on any given day in Hawaii, blows doors. His favorite adage is "Anybody can talk about getting radical but talk is cheap . . . you just got to do it!" It's all power surfing developed from a lifetime of riding Hawaiian waves. Gomes is renowned for being one of the only surfers in the world to consistently hit the lip at big Sunset. His backhand Pipe attack is even

AARON CHANG

more alarming for he has perfected the rail grab takeoff and gets as or more barreled than any goofyfooter out there.

So what of Tony Moniz and Marvin Foster? You don't see these guys busting down the door at any PSAA or APSA event. These guys live for hardcore surfing in places like Bali or Tahiti or Hawaii. No matter how many times Joe Wiggle wins the grovel pro he's going to come up against one of these explosive surfers in the Triple Crown and get trampled, Hawaiian style.

Look at what surfers like Buttons Kaluhiokalani, Mark Liddell and Larry Bertlemann have bestowed upon the sport. In the early stages of hotdogging these Hawaiian guys were the loosest, most innovative waveriders anywhere. Back in the days when a cutback into the foam was a radical move, these boys were cutting loose with laybacks, 360s and tail slides. Their Hawaiian styles made surfing look like hydro-acrobatic pleasure.

Other exceptional surfers like Sunny Garcia, Hans Hedemann and Derek Ho have mastered powerful Hawaiian surf as well as small-wave hotdogging to the point of upper-level world tour success. Both of the Hos, Mike and Derek, surf precisely and calculatedly. Couple this precision with nerves of steel, gut determination and Hawaiian power and you come up surfing like nowhere else on earth.

And so will it be as long as those gargantuan swells continue to avalanche. The ambience of Hawaiian surfing speaks for itself. It reeks of heritage and lives on through sheer attraction. There's a group of hau trees bordering the beach at Waikiki where the original Outrigger Canoe Club was created in the early 1900s. Long before that, young Hawaiians dragged their blessed handcarved planks down to shore and enjoyed what they loved. The tradition lives to this very day, for Hawaii will always be "home to the surfer . . ."

149

TONY NOLAN

Not all the good waves on Oahu are confined to the north shore. Ala Moana, left, is open for business all summer long. Right: Sunny Garcia, one of Hawaii's best.

JEFF HORNBAKER

Japan

THE SUN ALSO RISES

RYOJI KURIBAYASHI

translated by SHINO KIKUCHI

On the world maps used in the United States, America is located in the center and Japan in the far east. But we don't consider our country to be located in the far east – it is located in the center on maps we usually use which set Europe in the west and the United States in the east.

151

Japan is an island country made up of a strip of four big islands with the Pacific Ocean, the Nihon Kai, the East China Sea and the Sea of Okhotsk around the country. From north to south, there are Hokkaido, Honshu (the biggest island), Shikoku, Kyushu and Okinawa at the south end.

Since Japan is long and slender from north to south, in February you can enjoy skiing in the morning in below freezing temperatures in Hokkaido, and surfing in the afternoon in 68°F (20°C) in Okinawa.

The best surfing spots in Japan are along the coast of the Pacific and it is possible to surf almost everywhere along the coast. The best waves for surfing are before and after low-pressure weather patterns, and when a typhoon passes northwards along the Pacific coast.

Typhoons are a gift from nature for Japanese surfers, but for others they mean stormy weather and heavy rain, so we surfers usually cannot shout gleefully "A typhoon is coming!" Though it depends on each year's conditions, we average 25 typhoons a year from the end of July to November, with the best season being from August to October. During these months surfers travel from south to north according to the course the typhoon is taking and try to get the best waves out of the year's typhoons.

Want to see the keenest surfers in the world trying all the big new moves in good waves? Go to Niijima Island, Japan.

TSUCHIYA

All over the world nowadays, kids like to have stickers, stickers, stickers on their boards, wetsuits, wherever they can put 'em. These Japanese kids are on the case!

152

HISTORY OF *NAMINORI*

It is not known who the first surfers were in Japan. In Japanese, surfing is called *naminori*; *nami* means wave and *nori* means riding. It is believed that people were "riding waves" in the time of the Shogun (from the end of the twelfth century to the fourteenth century). In the literature of that time, there are descriptions of fishermen riding waves on a piece of wood, which seems similar to the bodyboarding of today.

In 1945, when Japan was under US occupation, many American soldiers stationed all over the country were surfing on Japanese beaches. These surfers are considered the first to have surfed in Japan and it was the beginning of modern surfing in our country.

In 1960 a Japanese boy met one of the GI surfers for the first time at Shonan Kaigan, about 35 miles (56 kilometers) southwest of Tokyo. They were carrying balsa surfboards made by the manufacturers Surfboards Hawaii, Gordon & Smith, Hobie and Hansen. There was a boy who made his own board, copied from *Surfer* magazine, designed by John Severson.

Since most of the Americans who were surfing at Shonan Beach were from California, one might safely say that a pioneer of modern surfing in Japan is Duke Kahanamoku, since it was the Duke who introduced surfing to California in the first place.

The first surfing contest in Japan was held at Kamogawa Beach, Chiba, in 1964, and was a qualifying round for the World Championships held in Australia in September, at which Tak Kawahara competed. In 1965 the Nippon Surfing Association (NSA) was founded.

Although we made a very good start in those pioneering days, as a nation we have still not realised our full surfing potential. And, unfortunately, a history of surfing in Japan since then shows that we seem to be doing things the hard way.

Japan has three surfing magazines – *Surfin' Life*, *Surfing World* and *Surfer* – three Association of Surfing Professionals (ASP) contests, and the Japan Pro Surfing Association (JPSA) holds six to eight contests a year. In spite of this, the social status of surfing and surfers in Japan is much lower than in the United States, Australia, and even countries where there are no ASP events.

From 1965, when the NSA was founded, to

1975, when pro surfing first began in Japan, surfing in our country has developed steadily. It was the dawn of surfing in Japan and the pioneers of this period, called the first generation of Japanese surfing, built its foundation.

In 1966 the NSA held the first All Japan Amateur Surfing Contest. Since then the contest has been held every year at various surf spots throughout Japan. The first contest was held at Kamogawa Beach in Chiba and Mikio Kawai was the winner. After the contest, the NSA started to establish branches all over the country and the number of surfers increased steadily.

In 1969 five Japanese surfers competed in the Makaha International Championship in Hawaii and

Top: Checking out Nagata, a clean left point that holds some seriously big waves around typhoon time. Bottom: Kamogawa, Chiba — site of Japan's first major national surf contest in 1966.

TSUCHIYA

Doji Isaka entered the fifth World Contest at Bells Beach, Australia, as the first Japanese competitor in 1970. Since the World Cup held at San Diego in 1972, to which the NSA sent Japanese surfers such as Mikio Kawai, Michio Degawa and Hiromi Isaka, there has been an active cultural exchange between foreign and Japanese surfers. We gained a great deal from the visits of foreign surfers like Mike Purpus, Gerry Lopez, Reno Abellira and David Nuuhiwa who surfed our waves and showed us what surfing was all about.

The Professional Surfing Association (now known as the JPSA) was founded in 1975 and some of the world's top surfers, such as Mark Richards, Wayne Bartholomew and Shaun Tomson, began to compete in Japan.

Then followed the best period in Japan's surfing history. After the foundation of the Professional Surfing Association, pro contests were held fre-

quently and the surfboard industry boomed. Many competitors were visiting the country from all over the world and the young people in Japan – surfers and non-surfers alike – began to admire and imitate the fashions and lifestyles of the surfers from California. They wore tee-shirts with "UCLA" printed on them, blue jeans, jogging shoes and so on. This was known as "West Coast fashion" in Japan. With this phenomenon as a background, surfing itself became a part of the fashion, followed by a fashion trend called "surfer's fashion." As a result, the number of surf shops, which formerly had only been in surf spots such as Shonan or Chiba, increased enormously.

Now, however, the Japanese surfing world has fallen on hard times. Gone are the brisk, flourishing days, and a large number of surf shops and factories have closed.

Although Japan is surrounded by ocean, most people do not have a real understanding of the ocean. Some school teachers tell their students to keep away from the waves because they are

International competitors love coming to Japan. They know it'll always be an adventure. **Below**: *John Shimooka flows through a ride at Hebara.* **Right**: *Hans Hedemann rips out a large slice of Niijima beach break.* **Far right**: *Japanese kids like the beach as much as anyone else.*

JEFF HORNBAKER

dangerous, and surfing's status as a sport is considered to be lower than yachting, diving and windsurfing. This is because some people joined the surfing boom in Japan only because it was trendy and part of a fashion fad of the time. They did not know or care what surfing was really all about and surfers who had a genuine love of the sport did not have a chance to let people know what a surfer really is.

Nevertheless, surfing has taken root in Japan and there are many new young surfers entering the sport. One can only hope that enough real surfers will survive the hard times and that, together with the growing number of young surf "rats," will establish a real surfing style and status in Japan — in this island country where "The Sun Also Rises."

JEFF HORNBAKER

Africa

A WAVE-HUNTING GROUND

JOHN ELLISS

Africa has staggering surf potential – most of it unrealized. The countries of the northwest, which were once under French colonial rule, have small surf communities and quite a few visiting surfers from France. Morocco is a regular extension of the European surf trip and Senegal is surfed regularly by French surfers.

Moving south, surfers become more of a rarity although Gambia, Guinea, Sierra Leone and the Ivory Coast have all been surfed at some stage. If you went there, however, chances are you'd be the only surfer in sight.

Little is known about surfing in Cameroon, Gabon or the Congo but rumours abound . . . Angola and Namibia were beginning to get some exposure in the surfing media during the early 70s but the wars of the last 15 years have seen tight restrictions placed on access for foreigners.

On the east coast, little is known of the surf outside South Africa. It's not until Kenya, around the town of Malindi, that an outside reef collects a lot of swell, producing waves in the occasional pass, but small beach breaks are the usual fare. Farther north, the island of Lamu, an Arab port founded in the fourteenth century, also receives a fair share of surf.

One of the factors contributing to the lack of surf exploration in Africa is the problem of road travel within many African nations. There's no guarantee that coastal areas will be served by a road of any type, and unless a town or major village is in the area, chances of access are remote.

There's all sorts of things to think about when surfing Africa — sharks, disease, cold water, travel problems and the like. Michael Barry samples the bright side of the Dark Continent.

159

PAUL SARGEANT

JOHN VEAGE

Aside from transport problems, dealing with the bureaucracies of developing nations is never fun and a great deal of patience is required. Visa requirements should be known well in advance and the necessary vaccinations should be documented. Cholera and yellow fever inoculations are a must as is a course of anti-malaria pills.

To escape sickness while traveling in Africa is rare, especially through regions where a surf search is likely to lead. Unboiled drinking water is to be avoided and immediate attention should be paid to cuts and infection. Hepatitis, diarrhoea and dysentery are common but common-sense and simple precautions help the traveler stay healthy.

Stay out of freshwater rivers and lakes – throughout Africa. Bilharzia, caused by tiny worms which are prevalent in stagnant water, can make you very sick. Swim in the ocean.

The ocean isn't totally safe, however, with sharks being a frequent worry along the east coast. Warm currents flowing north along the coast attract fish which in turn attract sharks, namely the Great White and the Zambesi, both quite aggressive. Attacks have happened quite often, particularly south of Durban in the waters off the Transkei, around East London and in the Jeffreys Bay area.

The largest surfing community is, of course, in South Africa, and in spite of all its social and political problems it has been a major attraction to international surfers for years. The reason is simple – it has a ridiculous abundance of waves of outstanding quality. The most consistent surf is found during winter, April through to September, although summer has its moments.

The main surfing centers are Durban, Cape Town and East London. Durban is the typical city

CHRIS VAN LENNEP

*They've been saying it for hundreds of years — Africa is a land of extremes. **Opposite top**: A West African rivermouth, yet to be surfed. **Left**: Pierre Tostee competing in front of a city crowd, Durban. **Right**: In South Africa, if you're black, you're really black.*

surf scene, the center of the industry and the most competitive area. The weather and water are warm all year and the place is very similar to Australia's Gold Coast. The latest surfing and fashion trends are followed closely here and the "hard core" surfers from other parts of the country often refer to the Durban surfers as mere "pretty boys."

South African surfing has played a major role in the international scene, being one of the original legs on the professional circuit. It has produced a number of world-class surfers as well as some major players on the administration side. Of these the leaders have come from Durban, namely Shaun Tomson and Peter Burness.

Burness, president of the Association of Surfing Professionals (ASP) since 1983, has been the driving force behind the professional scene in South Africa for a number of years and has largely been responsible for its development. His son Michael is a former Top 16 surfer.

Shaun Tomson has been the dominant performer in South African surfing since the early 70s. He is one of the sport's true leaders, having been world champion in 1977 and holding a place in the Top 16 for 13 consecutive years. To those outside South Africa he epitomizes South African

PAUL SARGEANT

JEFF DIVINE

THE DIVISIONAL COUNCIL OF THE CAPE
THIS BEACH FOR WHITES ONLY
BY ORDER SECRETARY

DIE AFDELINGSRAAD VAN DIE KAAP
HIERDIE STRAND SLEGS VIR BLANKES
OP LAS SEKRETARIS

JEFFREYS BAY

JOHN ELLISS

Only a handful of surf breaks in the world have legendary international status. Jeffreys Bay is one. It is regarded by many surfers as the best right hand-breaking wave in the world – and there are many stories, photos and films to support that opinion.

Jeffreys Bay is a point break south of Port Elizabeth on the southeastern coast of South Africa. It is surrounded by a small town of the same name, a town with a healthy surfing population attracted by the legendary waves. A long-breaking wave, it has eight different named sections, the major two being Supertubes and Impossibles.

Surfers from all over the world brave the cold winter conditions in an effort to catch the Antarctic-generated swells which produce the best waves. The surfing population of Jeffreys Bay explodes in the southern hemisphere's winter and on a cold July morning with a six-foot (1.8 meter) swell and offshore winds, up to 70 surfers may be in the lineup.

Many of the top professional surfers have made the trek to Jeffreys and none has been disappointed. South African Shaun Tomson, one of the world's best-ever surfers, honed his famous tube riding there.

Jeffreys has been the scene of some memorable performances, including some outstanding competitions. In July 1984, over a four-day event, the surf at Jeffreys ranged from four to 10 feet (one to three meters) with the world's best surfers reveling in perfect conditions.

Surf journalist Derek Hynd described the conditions as a surfer's dream. His enthusiasm went further as he watched

"IMPOSSIBLES"

"SUPERTUBES"

Sand and rocks

JEFFREYS BAY

PAUL SARGEANT

changed over the past 10 years, making it more difficult to link the different sections than in the past.

Taking off on a eight-foot (2.4 meter) wave at Jeffreys is filled with anticipation because you could be in for the biggest thrill of your life. The wall lines up in front of the surfer and the option is whether to look for the tube or go for some high-speed maneuvers on the face. When the wave is lining up properly and the sections are makeable, Jeffreys offers one of the longest rides in the world.

Sometimes the place defies description and throughout the years surfers have run out of superlatives in describing the wave and their feelings regarding it. Perhaps an indication lies in the words of Richard Marsh, a young Australian professional, "When you pull off some of those waves you can honestly say, 'Wow, that was better than sex.' "

Left: **O**ne of the best backhand surfers to hit J-Bay, Mark Occhilupo. **Below:** Just imagine paddling out.

the likes of Mark Occhilupo, Tom Carroll and a host of pro surfing up-and-comers "pull into the most incredible second point-break section imaginable . . . This was the world's best wave finally showing its merit."

Naturally, things have changed over the years and the village has grown considerably. The area is popular not only with surfers but with vacationers from the country's main centers. Much of the foreshore, which was once farmland, has been sold off and developed. Apparently the building and the removal of sand dunes has affected the amount of sand off the point and the lineup has

AARON CHANG

CHRIS VAN LENNEP

164

CHRIS VAN LENNEP

*T*wo sides of South African surfing. **A**bove: The boys survey the
cold ruggedness of Cape Town's Outer Kom. **Bottom**: The
grommets of Durban are as star-crazy as the kids in Sydney or
Huntington Beach.

surfing, and to those within that surfing community
he is the one they most admire and emulate.

Shaun, dubbed "The Boss," is a product of
Durban. He is a city boy – articulate, well edu-
cated, stylish and sophisticated. He is very aware
of his role as an ambassador for South African surfing and professional surfing in general.

Surfers from Cape Town, East London and the
areas south of Port Elizabeth see themselves as
more "dedicated," putting up with cold water and
isolation but getting out there regardless. The South
African surf community is hospitable and foreign
surfers are usually greeted with enthusiasm.

Surfing in Cape Town is a unique experience
– freezing water, big solid waves and landscapes
of amazing grandeur. With a car a surfer has
access to both sides of the Cape of Good Hope,
which means that a surfable wave can almost
always be found within a 45-minute drive of the
city. The breaks in the area range from mellow
beach breaks at Table View and Long Beach to the
very meaty reef breaks like the Outer Kom and
Crayfish Factory.

One of Durban's hottest, Gavin Swart, just leans himself back into a Bellito barrel.

In Durban the main breaks are centrally located, with the Bay of Plenty, Dairy Beach and South Beach virtually next to each other. The only exception is Cave Rock, a powerful righthand reef, which is about 20 minutes' drive south of the city. Further south there are many breaks within a return day's trip of Durban although sharks can be a worry.

East London has a variety of breaks and a dedicated surf community, the one which spawned women's champion Wendy Botha. Nahoon Reef is a favorite with the locals but, once again, sharks are a problem.

The coastal strip running southwest from Port Elizabeth to Cape Agulhes is where some of the country's best surf is found. Jeffreys Bay and Cape St Francis, two of the world's most famous breaks, are located in this region. Every surfer should try to surf this area at least once in his or her life.

The variety of people, cultures, climate, wildlife, terrain and vegetation make Africa a remarkable continent. For a surfer this is intensified by the possibility of surfing some of the most untamed and remote areas of the world. The possibility of being the first surfer to do so makes it that much more attractive, something which may offset the inevitable hassles.

Europe
CIVILIZED SURF

WAYNE RABBIT BARTHOLOMEW

Not long ago, people could not comprehend the image of excellent waves rolling along European beaches. Surfing the waves off the historically famous coastlines of France, Cornwall, Scotland and Spain just did not seem a possibility.

One of the world's modern, dynamic sports being practised amid ancient relics has conjured up a romantic spirit of adventure amongst surfers the world over. The chance to ride waves in the pirate coves of Penzance, or to take off on a reef whose ancient foundations were made even more prominent courtesy of a sunken treasure ship is unique to a sport whose image is synonymous with exotic locations such as Bali, Hawaii and Tahiti.

Surfing has, in fact, been enjoyed for nearly 30 years in certain parts of Europe. From humble beginnings, pioneers such as the Sumpter brothers of Britain, Frenchmen Barland and Jean-Marie Latigau plus Welshman Pete Jones have made major contributions to the development of the sport, introducing the Malibu board and the surfing lifestyle to continental shorelines.

As the first surfing boom engulfed California and Australia in the 60s, Europe remained in isolation, totally undiscovered apart from the odd excursion into the unknown by the small group of surfing pioneers.

The Kombi van unlocked the doorway to hidden treasures and as word inevitably trickled back to the US and "Down Under," the first bohemian hordes descended upon the European wavefields. Inexplicably, the pilgrimage dwindled after that

With their fiery character and natural athleticism, Spaniards will make some great surfers in the years to come. This kid, Jorge Imbery, may be the first of a new crew to tackle the world pro circuit.

first onslaught, leaving Europe unscathed and relatively empty through the 70s.

My first sip of European culture in 1976 was to have a long-lasting aftertaste, and as is the case with many first-time experiences at incredible outposts, the historical value made for a memorable stint. Far from being the international pioneer, I was seven years behind Nat Young and Wayne Lynch, but the fact that Jeff Hakman had been the last universally recognized surfer to visit France four years before I set foot on French soil made the experience even more novel.

The reality of civilized waves was driven home early. Long lines of solid swell were clearly visible as the 727 paralleled the southwest coast of France. The straight, white beaches were in stark contrast to the thick pine forests that lined the coast, gradually filtering into lush green valleys dotted with farmhouses. Out of the east, the land began to rise, gently at first then sheer as the mighty Pyrénées rose from the clouds.

To the surfing connoisseur, the European lifestyle can be truly savored only by completely scouring the many thousands of miles that comprise the surfable coastlines of France, Spain, Portugal and the UK. In England, the traditional port of entry being Heathrow, the done thing for each generation of wave-hunters has been to buy a van in London and head south, but not before giving jolly old England a good going-over.

The Cornish coast, and in particular the southwest corner along the boot of Cornwall, offers the best foothold the surfing lifestyle has established in "the mother country." The craggy cliffs and hidden coves were once notorious for pirate smuggling, and many treasure-laden ships have been pirated, or came to grief courtesy of an errant beacon on a cliff, along this coast. But nowadays Penzance and other former pirate haunts like St Agnes have become the playground for the nation's youth, offering fairly consistent surf and plenty of nightlife.

168

Wales has waves – or at least that section of coast not blotted out by Ireland. For sure, the further one gets to the North Pole the more dedicated one must be to the surfing cause, but the alienation that accompanies a trip to United Kingdom outposts melts away under the compounded warmth of these amazing surfing fraternities, plus a few pints of beer, of course.

At first, the very thought of a surfing expedition to Scotland seems ridiculous, but again nature, in conjunction with the elements, creates small pockets of coastline favorable to surfing. The ever-swirling North Sea has carved huge, inaccessible cliffs into Scotland's west coast, yet the area around Thurso not only acts as a sanctuary from the raging, windswept ocean swells, but also offers some very decent reef breaks and rocky headlands. Amazingly, a warmer Gulf Stream holds the icy North Sea at bay, allowing surfers to take to the water for most of the year in reasonably comfortable conditions.

JEFF HORNBAKER

JEFF HORNBAKER

Those clean, airbrushed French beach breaks can drive a surfer mad. **Above**: *Sunny Garcia needs no excuse to give this wave a hiding.* **Left**: *Ted Robinson gazes down the barrel of a six-foot (1·8-meter) cannon.*

Parts of Ireland's west coast resemble a veritable surfing oasis. One just could not imagine subtropical jungles and hollow, challenging reef breaks in Ireland, but being completely open to the seemingly permanent low-pressure systems that hang out off Iceland, and the accompanying hard offshore winds, gives one an eerie feeling of actually being in the forgotten valley.

To the south, the Bay of Biscay cuts into the coast like two sides of a parallelogram, the French coast facing west and the Spanish coast facing northwest, providing a funnel for the massive swells generated by the Atlantic Ocean. In fall and winter, masses of cold Arctic air move southeast across Alaska and Canada, and as they meet the Atlantic the air begins to swirl, giving birth to deep low-pressure systems, which in turn begin to churn the sea. Storm-born swells begin rolling towards the continent and over several thousand miles they form into columns, molding into a semblance of order as they heave to their final destination.

The deep Atlantic trenches that lie just off the coast of southwest France restrict the softening effect of the continental shelf on the ocean swells, so that the beach breaks of Hossegor and Cap Breton are the most powerful outside Hawaii. Although now considered a playground for the serious surfer, the hollow, grinding, beach breaks of Hossegor were once considered too dangerous, and even today the crowd becomes very thin once the swell reaches eight feet (2.5 meters) plus.

JEFF HORNBAKER

JEFF HORNBAKER

Another unique feature of the Hossegor coast is surfing in between and amongst a backdrop of giant crumbling bunkers that serve as a reminder of the days of German occupation. At La Piste a dozen bunkers have been herded together like marbles, testimony to some hideous winter storm since the Second World War.

Biarritz, a quaint coastal city nestled into the southwest corner of France, is where the free spirits of summer converge for the famous beach lifestyle. Yet Biarritz is also a stronghold of the Basque separatist, and a fairly possessive local surfing populace.

*If you really want to get to know French surf, it helps to hang around for a while and feel out its power. **Above**: James "Chappy" Jennings has hung around and reaps the rewards regularly. **Opposite**: Arsene Harehoe, all the way from Tahiti.*

When the swell passes the 10-foot (three-meter) mark, the reefs and points of Biarritz come into their own. Lafitania is a rocky point, just to the south of the city center, and when Hossegor is in a state of "victory at sea," clean 8- to 10-foot (two- to three-meter) swells hit the outside ledge and wrap beautifully into Lafitania. Just to the south lies Guéthary, a Sunset-like reef break that remains

HOSSEGOR

PETER WILSON

The popularity of surfing in France has increased dramatically in recent years. Although the coastline has only a small quantity of reef and point breaks, any deficiency is more than compensated for by some of the best medium-sized beach breaks to be found anywhere in the world.

The coastline in the southwest corner of France is the most consistent area for surf. In one continuous 200-mile (320-kilometer) strip, stretching from Lacanau-Océan in the north to the Bidassor River on the Spanish border in the south, there are so many different surf breaks that they are known only by their locality rather than by specific names.

The Hossegor area is one such place. In reality it is a 12-mile (20-kilometer) stretch of coast taking in the towns of Capbreton, Hossegor and Seignosse. The waves are fast, powerful and hollow — the source of many enjoyable hours of

"tube time." They also provide the basis for many excellent surfing stories. After witnessing the near-perfect barrels, nobody is going to question the tales of Tom Curren disappearing into a 100-yard-long barrel in August of 1988, or how Occhilupo was tubed for an unbelievable 14 seconds in October of 1989. Stories such as these pass through the surfing world and add to the mystique of surfing Hossegor.

A number of expatriates from Australia and America have made a home in the region. In surfing terms, Hossegor is to France what Torquay is to Australia and Malibu is to the States. The analogy is not due to the presence of the Rip Curls or the Quiksilvers, although they have both opened in the region, but to the quality of the surf itself.

The best surfing conditions are during the northern hemisphere's summer and

HOSSEGOR

*F*or a sandbar break, Hossegor does not play games. **A**bove left: On a big swell waves break well out to sea. **B**ottom left: Maurice Cole looks for the tube. **B**elow: Sebastian St Jean finds it — a lot of it.

providing a closeup inspection of the bottom for the unwary surfer.

Surfing is not the only place a person can do him- or herself some harm. The summer vacation lifestyle can be responsible for even greater damage. The streets of Hossegor are lined with numerous cafés and bars, inexpensive restaurants and some outrageous nightclubs. During the season Hossegor becomes a young person's town. In late August Hossegor is one of the stops on the lucrative European leg of pro

surfing's world tour. The Rip Curl Pro Landes surfing event draws crowds in excess of 100,000 people, so don't expect too many uncrowded waves while the pro tour is around; but do expect the night-time party programs to step up a notch or two.

Hossegor, July through to November, offers the traveling surfer everything he or she could need — excellent waves, good food and a cross between the traditional and vacation lifestyle of the French. A word of warning though: don't hang around too long after November as the water cools down rapidly, the ocean is racked by severe gales and there is every chance you could be walking on snow-covered beaches to reach the waves.

early fall. (This has stretched into winter in recent years.) Although the summer period is vacation time in Europe and the resorts are packed, it is easy to walk onto the beach and find an uncrowded peak producing left and right barrels. If the peak eventually becomes crowded, all you have to do is walk a short distance up or down the beach. There is every chance of finding an equally good bank with nobody out there.

Perhaps all this sounds too good to be true, but there are down sides to surfing in the region. The tidal changes are extreme, sometimes as much as nine feet (three meters), and consequently surf conditions change not by the day or week but by the hour. An example of this is a bank that could look like junk for days and then become the best surf spot on the coast in a matter of hours. Of course the opposite is also true.

If you are thinking of including Hossegor on the itinerary of your next surfing trip to Europe, don't be deceived by the "beach-break" tag. The swells that are generated somewhere in the mid-Atlantic pack a board-snapping punch and are quite capable of

JEFF HORNBAKER

composed up to, and sometimes beyond, 16 feet (five meters).

Alcion is a classic left-breaking reef at the southern end of the bay, that needs a considerable swell to kick-start, and then gets mechanical as the nearly protruding reef redirects the peaking swells down its contours.

As the swell passes the 10-foot (three-meter) mark, it's time to head south of the border, deeper into Basque country. Once past the frontier into Spain the changes are swift and dramatic. Not only is the countryside different but the entire pace changes – the Spanish live life in a higher gear than all their neighbors, and it's important to keep pace.

Most of Spain is uncrowded, undiscovered and unexploited, and the locals like to keep it that way, but in hushed tones over a café grande they speak of places to the south, big-wave locations and rivermouths in the Mundaka mold. The Spanish surfers, being naturally free-spirited and openly friendly, are keen to share these new frontiers with their foreign friends, but also reluctant to allow the photographers to document their secret waves.

A full day's drive through the broiling heat of Spain and you reach the rugged land of northern Portugal. The winding roads, whilst slowing the pace, showcase spectacular backdrops of deep gorges, green valleys and sheer cliffs.

*The professionals love coming to Europe. **Above left**: Hans Hedemann warms up. **Above**: Barton Lynch surrounded by the locals. **Opposite**: Tom Carroll unpacks his boards in a picturesque place. **Below**: Todd Holland prepares to discover a very picturesque place.*

JEFF HORNBAKER

The pace of life again changes in Portugal, the locals content to go with a much mellower flow than the French or Spanish. The Portuguese are generally the friendliest of the European surfing community – perhaps their isolation and surfing infancy make them more open to welcoming the traveling surfer as a novel experience.

Portugal is a surfer's dream come true. Super-cheap living, great food, especially the seafood, and a stable, war-free environment make for a pleasant, inexpensive stay. The real treat is the fact that the place is jampacked with world-class waves, and, jutting further west, picks up the lion's share of swells from many aspects.

Peniche is the home of Portuguese surfing. It's where the fathers of the sport set up camp and introduced surfing in the 60s; it's the home of a world-class wave, Supertubes, a faultless left that rivals the great beach breaks of the world.

The Portuguese surfers are eager to host traveling surfers, the hardest decision being in which direction to head, Peniche being dead center in the surfable coastline. Legendary underground breaks to the north are cloaked in secrecy, but the surf breaks several hours' south of Peniche are considered the best in the land.

The Ericiera area is rich in wave bounty, an endless stream of excellent reef and point breaks. Further south, where the coast abruptly turns back in towards Lisbon, the coastal town of Cascais is

175

MUNDAKA

PETER WILSON

Since the beginning of the "soul surfing" era in the early 70s, Europe has gradually become a favorite for the traveling surfer. Depending on the time of the year, the trail runs from France to Morocco taking in the coasts of Spain and Portugal. One break on the trail has become legendary. Nestled amongst the hilly slopes of a small cove, the tiny Spanish fishing village of Mundaka, deep in Basque country, lends its name to one of the finest rivermouth surf breaks in Europe, and possibly the world.

Mundaka has gained its reputation partly because it rarely breaks — when it does, though, the waves are nothing short of classic. It takes a massive storm high up in the North Atlantic to generate swells through to the Bay of Biscay.

Mundaka lies at the vertex of the right angle which forms the north coast of Spain and the west coast of France. The angles of the coastline thus act as a funnel for the approaching swells. Up to six feet (1.8 meters) Mundaka is forgiving, but when the waves push towards the eight to 10 feet (2.4 to three meters) mark, conditions approach Hawaiian proportions. The swells pushing in are often fanned by howling offshore winds channeled by the river valley. The river itself flows straight through the peak, often adding another dimension to the takeoff.

Paddling into the wave, one is often blinded by the spray, hoping that at some stage down the face a rail will set. From there, it is a ride of varying sections. The barrel begins almost straight away and doesn't let up for over 30 or 40 yards (27 or 37 meters). It does back off for a short time before the speed

JOLI

Mundaka looks a lot mellower than it is. The pretty town, its pleasant harbor, the quiet lapping of waves — and the sudden appearance of a huge, explosive wave. Left: Wayne Lynch sets it up. Above: What could be sweeter?

is required again. The rides last for as long as you can handle the pace. Without a doubt, there will be a walloping by shut-down sections, but if you are lucky enough to escape, you can ride for 200 yards (180 meters) or more if your legs hold out.

Village life at Mundaka seems to have been moving at the same pace for years. The port is home to a fleet of small wooden fishing boats — commercial fishing seems to have passed Mundaka by. Most of the fishermen are in their late 50s or early 60s, and on the days of no swell they steer their boats through the gap in the sea wall and out to the fishing grounds. When the swells come, the men spend their time deep in conversation,

sipping strong black coffee at the bars and cafés that line the port.

Tall three- or four-storey buildings are clustered together, with the narrow roadways or cobbled paths between them winding their way through the village. It is far easier and quicker to walk than to drive the narrow one-way roads. A large Catholic church dominates the landscape overlooking the break, and topics of discussion to avoid with the locals are, of course, religion and politics.

The Basque ambience and culture are overpowering. The culture has unknown origins, and the people have their own language and are battling for an independent state. A militant separatist movement has claimed responsibility for shootings and car-bombings during its fight with the Spanish government. The traveling surfer is usually safe from the conflicts, and these elements add another dimension to surfing what may be the best rivermouth break in the world.

MUNDAKA

TOWNSHIP

Rivermouth

JOLI

located. The domain of the young at heart, Cascais is where the cool crew hang out at the various beach bars and nightclubs after dark and either surf the local breaks by day or head towards Ericiera looking for the value.

Lisbon is nestled about 30 miles (50 kilometers) east of Cascais, and it offers a picturesque blend of old and new, a must to complete one's culturization. A rare wave rolls down the river by the harbor in certain conditions, and a sense of historical significance overcame me as I stood overlooking the point where Vasco da Gama and Bartholomew Diaz embarked on their great voyages of discovery.

Though geographically not a part of Europe, Morocco is steeped in surfing history, the legendary Ankar Point a timeless destination for any surfer seeking to fulfill the European experience. Set in northern Africa just over the Mediterranean, opposite Gibraltar, Morocco offers a unique experience in surfdom. Ankar Point is another of the classic meeting grounds, where surfers squat and

AARON CHANG

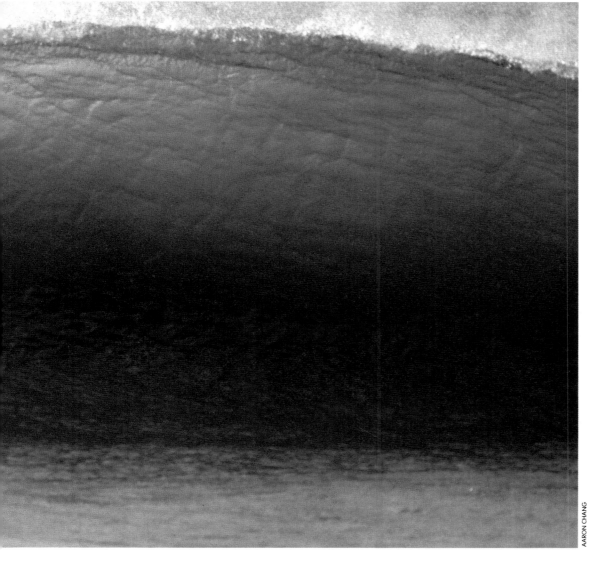

AARON CHANG

Magoo Dela Rosa is one of Peru's finest surfers. He cruises the world looking for fun on the pro tour, but it's back at home where he finds the space to relax and surf like a local.

In the twentieth century surfing developed around the world. While in North America and Australia it experienced rapid growth, in South America it progressed at a more sluggish pace. There are no precise dates, but it is believed that the first South American surfers appeared around the 1930s in Brazil and Peru. By the late 60s the Peruvians were the continent's top surfers, and when one of them, Felipe Pomar, became world champion in 1965, South America definitely entered the international surfing scene. The quality of the waves in Peru and the skill of the Peruvian

AARON CHANG

AARON CHANG

Brazil is the center of South American surfing, with all the major surfing events and by far the biggest surfing population. There are still plenty of good moments to be had there by yourself, though.
Left: Peter King slots into one of them.
Opposite below: A rare reef break goes off.

The tribe grew more numerous and spread throughout the world quite fast. In the 70s surfing boomed as a lifestyle in Brazil. Rio's beaches saw an increasing number of surfers, with their trademark long hair and flower-patterned jeans. The rapid growth of South American surfing was a result of the joint effort of Brazilians and Peruvians. It was the Brazilians who brought to the continent the first professional surfing events, through the now-defunct IPS (International Professional Surfing).

Rio's Arpoador Beach became synonymous with surfing in the 70s. As the years went by, surfers searched for new points in South America, and countries such as Argentina, Uruguay, Chile and Ecuador became new alternatives in the continent. South American surfing expanded its boundaries. In Brazil, surfers left the beaches of Rio for those in the northeast and the south. Around this time the beaches of Santa Catarina State and Fernando de Noronha Island were the two major discoveries on the continent's Atlantic coast. Meanwhile, the first expeditions to Ecuador and Chile gave definite proof that the Pacific coast's surfing potential was not limited to Peru.

The 80s saw the final consolidation of surfing as a professional sport in Brazil. But elsewhere in South America surfriding still lagged behind the rest of the world. As the 90s begin, frontiers are not yet well drawn, and each day new points are discovered on both coasts. The northern part of the Atlantic coast remains a mystery, and the Brazilian north, the waves of French Guiana, Surinam, Guyana and Venezuela are still unsurfed. On the Pacific side, discovering Chile has become · the continent's newest adventure, while Ecuador and Colombia are *terra incognita* in the map of contemporary surfing.

surfers of the time were famous in South America and worldwide. Meanwhile, in other South American countries the fame of Peru's gigantic, perfect waves spread quickly. Thus many surfers, Brazilians in particular, began to visit Peruvian beaches, always in search of the perfect wave. Chicama became the Mecca of South American surf, while the righthanders of Punta Rocas were the competitive arena. Some of the most famous surfing competitions of the period were held in Punta Rocas, international events that attracted surfers from Australia, Hawaii, California and elsewhere.

CHICAMA

JOHN VEAGE

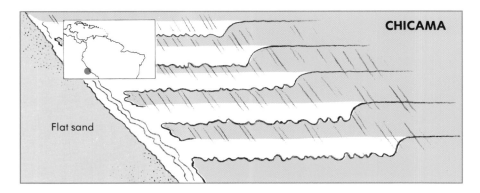

CHICAMA

Flat sand

Puerto Chicama is a nondescript, decaying fishing village on Peru's far north coast. A lifetime from Lima, the nation's capital, Chicama lies smack in the middle of the arid coastal desert belt. Here rainfall averages don't exist, and only the distant Andes provide any visual relief. But for the surfer this small town has a special significance.

The clarity of dawn was fading as I stood alone on the cliff's edge. The morning offshore breeze fanned the six-foot (two-meter) swell as it peaked off the sand point below me, and blew the tops off the throwing lips as the waves followed their predetermined path half a mile down into the bay.

Nothing had prepared me for this sight, a few photos in magazines, a couple of third-hand oral reports. It was perfect. I shouted, screamed, laughed and jumped up and down all at the same time. I shot two rolls of film in two minutes, expecting the crowds of surfers to appear at any moment, who never

did. The site was priceless, gone were the dramas, costs and ordeals of getting here, which were many and frequent.

I surfed for six hours, three hours by myself, until a handful of locals drifted in and out of the lineup. The heat of the desert and the cold waters of the Humboldt current that plies this coast don't make this ideal surfing conditions, but only a foolish person would have call to complain. The walk back to the takeoff position after a couple of long waves took me all of 15 minutes.

I surfed here for three days until the swell disappeared from whence it came. The worst wetsuit rash of my life, and a body that felt like one of the walking dead were a legacy of surfing here, but the most must be made of any chances.

Chicama is really two point breaks – the far outside point attracts and bends

the swell into the open bay, then the offshores and sand patterns form and line up the swell lines, so when it hits the inside point it peaks and pinwheels endlessly along the curve of the bay. Each wave is a replica of the one before and the one after.

Puerto Chicama is now privileged to have its own surf camp, which helps enormously for accommodation, food and safety, all of which are scratchy at best. This is a country where it pays to be careful.

The conditions that Chicama needs are not everyday occurrences, and it is not perfect 365 days of the year. Far from it. You need a little luck and a lot of perseverance, but those who are prepared to wait for the right conditions are assured of surfing one of the wonders of the surfing world.

The Chicama left is confusing just by its very length. What would you do? Take off, surf for 100 yards and flick off for a rest? Go move for move until your legs collapsed? Or just keep going till you got to the beach, ready for the 15-minute jog back to the takeoff?

HANK

Indonesia
THE LAST FRONTIER

PETER WILSON

Over the last two decades, Bali has been like a magnet, drawing surfers from all around the world. It has now become the first stepping stone to the rest of the Indonesian Archipelago. Surfers have been exploring and surfing isolated spots throughout the islands, but the known breaks are still only the tip of the iceberg.

Australian surfers and film-makers opened the eyes of the rest of the surfing world to the potential of surf in Bali and the rest of Indonesia. During 1970 the late Bob Evans, surf film-maker and founding editor of *Australian Surfing World* magazine, received reports from a Qantas steward about the waves around the Denpasar airport on Bali.

In August 1971 Bob took young Narrabeen surfers Mark Warren and Col Smith to Indonesia in search of waves. The result was the film *Family Free*, featuring Mark and Col enjoying the waves of Kuta Reef.

Shortly afterwards Albie Falzon (who had worked for Evans) and David Elfick produced *Morning of the Earth*. This film showed a young American, Rusty Miller, and an Australian gremmie, Stephen Cooney, paddling out into an ocean stacked with barreling lefthanders which seemed to peel for ever and ever.

During the filming of *Morning of the Earth*, Albie Falzon had been doing his own scouting of the area. Riding a motorbike he would follow dirt tracks as far as he could go before setting off on foot across fields and through prickly undergrowth. Each time he would be stopped by sheer cliffs. At

189

*S*ometimes just getting by in Bali can be difficult. Get a case of Bali belly, for instance, and suddenly the Third World can look a lot less glamorous. But as long as you can still pull into a beautiful green Padang Padang tube, everything turns out okay.

the base of the cliffs were uneven coral reefs running parallel to the shoreline which appeared to offer a variety of surf, but reaching them seemed impossible.

Albie finally found a dried-up watercourse which led into the mouth of a cave. The cave in turn emptied into the sea. The next day Albie returned with surfers and camera gear. The footage captured shows the cave and a break they called Uluwatu. The images would be etched into the minds of thousands of surfers forever.

Falzon and Elfick were also the founding editors of what has become the bible of Australian surfing magazines – *Tracks*. The pair promoted **Morning of the Earth** through the pages of their

magazine and helped spread the word of amazing waves and the fascinating lifestyle to be found on the tropical island of Bali.

The formula was continued a few years later by film-makers and photographers Dick Hoole and Jack McCoy. They spent months in Indonesia gathering material for **In Search of Tubular Swells**, which featured legendary Hawaiian Gerry Lopez. During this time, with the assistance of Doug

Indonesia is all about exploring — getting to new and strange places however you can, just to ride some fantastic waves. **Opposite top**: *Just the jeep ride on Nias can give you nightmares.* **Opposite below**: *The view on the track to Uluwatu.* **Below**: *Hiro Koutsusa tastes the sweetness of a successful west Java surf mission.*

TED GRAMBEAU

191

Warbrick and Brian Singer of Rip Curl fame and Michael Gordon, a journalist for the **Age** newspaper in Melbourne, they published the surfing magazine **Backdoor**. Though the magazine was short-lived, it helped promote both the film and the surfing potential of Bali.

With the mass of evidence about the perfect waves and easy accessibility of Bali, the rush was on. The rush was supported by the Indonesian government who mounted a worldwide campaign to sell the attractions of the tropical island paradise to wealthy tourists. But the campaign succeeded in attracting also an influx of not-so-wealthy surfers. In a country where the average annual per capita income was less than one hundred dollars, it was possible for a surfer of humble means to live like a king for months on end.

While the government promoted the four-star hotels on the Sanur side of the island, the small

JOLI

PETER SIMONS

The world's ultimate wave? It's hard to say. But if you could take all the best, from Jeffreys Bay to Sunset Beach, and put them together, Grajagan would stand up pretty well. **Above**: The bowl at Speed Reef. **Right**: Tom Carroll relaxes within G-Land's bowels. **Opposite**: The boat ride in gets you in the holiday mood.

GRAJAGAN

TOM CARROLL

Grajagan, on the southeastern tip of Java, is one of those surf spots that every surfer dreams of visiting. In 1988 I got my chance, and I was anything but disappointed.

My friends had been hyping me for years on this place. They'd had time to go there during long holidays to Bali, riding fantastic Indonesian swells while I was busy competing around the world in (usually) small, dribbly surf. ''It's insane!'' they'd say. ''You'll get the longest barrel of your life! You'll need a good long board.'' I was worried about getting hurt, but they said forget it – you won't, it's easier than that other great Indonesian wave, Uluwatu. I found *that* a bit hard to believe.

Years ago I learned not to anticipate

good surf. The ocean can be fickle and if you expect waves and don't get them it can be very depressing. But human nature took over and as we waited in Kuta Beach, Bali, for the bus to the mainland, I was feeling pretty revved up.

The trip to Grajagan is a crusher, eight hours in a tiny bus or ''bemo,'' followed by an anxious two-hour boat trip at the hands of uncertain Indonesian fishermen.

When we got there and I saw the lineup I realized that everything my friends had said was true.

Tavarua in Fiji is similar, but I've never ridden a wave that comes on to a coral reef in quite the same way as the Grajagan left. Maybe Padang Padang on Bali, but it doesn't have the length of ride. You have to get speed up as soon as you take off and hold that speed for the whole ride, or you've got no chance. It's important to be aware of that inside reef, especially at low tide, because it could leave you high and dry.

We wore little reef shoes for the 200-yard (180-meter) walk across coral to

the jump-off point, and tucked them into the waistbands of our board shorts once we were clear of the reef.

If I could give any advice on how to deal with the wave, it would be this: make sure you have a couple of very good boards that you've learned to surf well on at other locations. Strange and brilliant things happen on Grajagan waves, and if you're not used to your board you may not be ready for them. I remember one wave in particular, on a perfect sunny afternoon when only three of us hit the water. I took off on my first wave, pulled into the tube and rode right along the top of the foam – still inside the tube! It carried me through the whole wave without touching the lip. I just had to squat slightly and watch in amazement.

Surfers have been visiting Grajagan for nearly 20 years, but surfing there is still an adventure. You're out in the middle of nowhere in a totally foreign place, amid the jungle. It's very different from what most surfers are used to. And the waves are so much better!

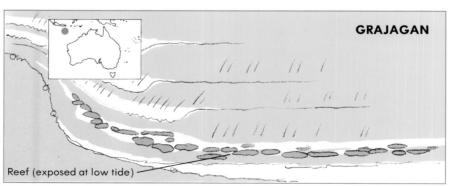

GRAJAGAN

Reef (exposed at low tide)

Indonesian surf camps are a strange mix of the comatose and the wildly intense. **Left**: An afternoon surf or a nap? **Opposite**: Darren Handley wonders if there's a way out of this Periscope Point cylinder.

DICK HOOLE

194

fishing village of Kuta offered traditional accommodation, including breakfast, for as little as fifty cents a night. What more could a surfer want? A tropical climate, crystal-clear water, an abundance of excellent waves, cheap food and lodgings and friendly people who were prepared to carry your board and massage your tired body for a pittance.

Before long the family-style losmens grew into small hotels, the traditional warungs (food stalls) turned into restaurants and the once tiny bars, where surfers gathered to discuss their day's exploits, developed into Western-style discos.

Regardless of the changes taking place, the Balinese remained true to their culture and religious beliefs. They accepted the Western influence but added their own flair. This was especially so in the food department. Spaghetti bolognese without the bolognese, or muesli which consisted of fresh fruit, yoghurt and nuts, or the once very popular dish, the special omelette. The "special" ingredient being the famous magic mushrooms — very popular for the mid-afternoon snack to ensure a good high in time for the spectacular Kuta Beach sunsets.

In a land renowned for its lefthanders, the goofyfooter rose in prominence. Hawaiian Gerry Lopez became a regular Indonesian traveler. First

at Uluwatu and later at the surf camp of G-Land on the coast of Java. The fast hollow lefts suited his style perfectly and after nearly 15 years he still returns each year to surf the waves of Grajagan. Newcastle's Peter McCabe became Lopez's surfing partner and at one stage earned the nickname of "Java Man" for his fondness for the isolated jungle waves.

Queenslander Thornton Fallander chose travel adventures and the waves of Indonesia over a life on the Association of Surfing Professionals (ASP) world tour. Fallander and Joe Engle starred in the Hoole/McCoy film **Riders on the Storm** which proved there was a righthander of world-class standard in the islands of Indonesia.

Jim Banks is another seasoned traveler and big-wave rider. In 1981 he won an inaugural ASP event in Bali, the Om Bali Pro held at Uluwatu.

Kim "Fly" Bradley from Avalon on Sydney's northern beaches was one of the few natural-footers to fall in love with Bali. Fly started traveling to the island in 1974. By 1977 he was virtually living there, shaping surfboards and trying to establish a local board-manufacturing industry.

Australians Dave Wiley and David Thomas are two names that have not had much media attention but they are credited with a great deal of the

TED GRAMBEAU

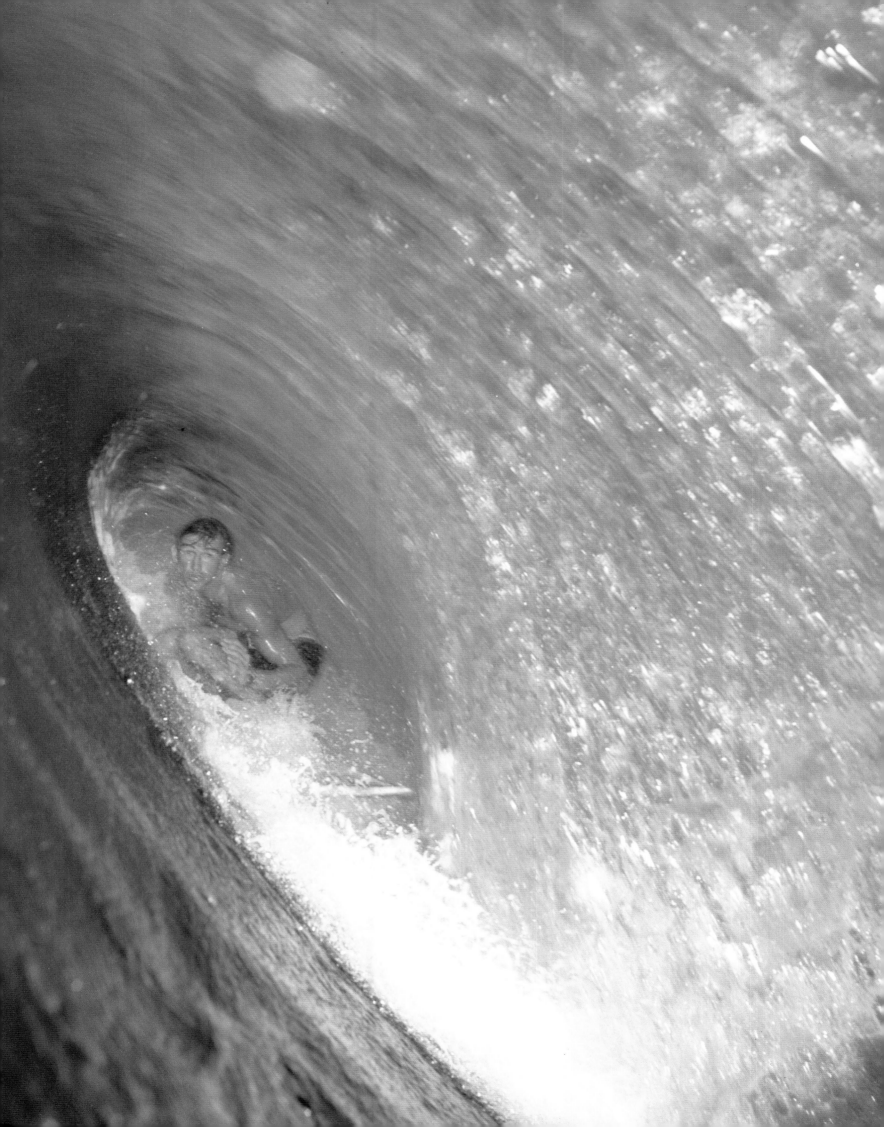

early exploration by people in the know. At one stage they were black-banned by the Indonesian authorities who considered them Fretilin spies after one trip through Timor in search of waves.

A further list of names should include Richard Harvey, Rick Neilsen, Jeff Hackman, Rusty Miller, Mike Boyum, who opened the first surf camp at Grajagan, Dick Von Straalen, Wayne Lynch and Terry Fitzgerald, who still regularly travel to Indonesia in search of empty waves.

The influence of surfing also extended to the local Balinese, which was surprising considering the average Hindu Balinese would rarely swim in the ocean. The sea was considered to hold evil monsters and the spirits of their dead. Made Kasim and Ketut Menda are two Balinese surfers who have made a name for themselves in the international arena.

Fifteen years ago Legian was the next beach down from Kuta and a totally separate village. Today, both villages have spread to the extent that it is hard to tell where Kuta finishes and Legian begins. This development has taken its toll. The

Nias, *above*, is a terrific place. As long as, *below*, you don't get cut open and have to submit to some friendly camp surgery.

BRIAN HUGHES

area is nowhere near as relaxed as it used to be. The trend now is to use Kuta and Legian as a base before heading off to other islands in search of waves.

Nias, Java and Nusa Lembongan had been the most common destinations, but with the influx of surfers from Japan, Brazil and Europe, and the continual stream of surfers from Australia and America, the well-known spots suffered from overcrowding. Uluwatu is rarely surfed by less than 30 wave-hungry travelers, and the presence of two Grajagan surf camps has led to as many as 40 guys in the water at G-Land. Even the corporate giant Coca-Cola has traveled to Nias in search of the perfect wave to film a television commercial.

A result of the crowding has been exploration further afield. Breaks have been discovered on Lombok, Sumbawa, Sumba, Flores and Timor, and

People often come back from Bali complaining about crowds, prices and commercialization . . . no wonder they feel like they're missing something. Bali Straits.

the exploration is continuing off the coast of Sumatra. Since not everyone has the time or resources to set out in search of uncrowded waves, an enterprising company, King Surfaris, established the packaged Indonesian Surfari.

The surf adventure sounds very exciting, but it is wise to take precautions against malaria and other tropical diseases. The isolation, razor-sharp coral reefs, sharks, tigers, snakes and the natural hazards of the jungle all pose problems for a surfer.

As a surfing location Indonesia's full potential might never be realized, but there is enough surf in Indonesia for everyone, all you need to do is go and find it.

Surf Culture

A SERIOUS SUBCULTURE

PAUL HOLMES

In an age when all kinds of fads and fashions have the pretense of being "lifestyles," surfing has been the real thing — a serious subculture — ever since the 1950s.

The 50s were the golden age of surfing. If the idea of renaissance is appropriate to surfing's history, the period from 1954 to 1964 represents that stage in its development. During this brief, 10-year epoch, surfing defined itself, lost its innocence, gained mass acceptance and, according to many soul-surfing cynics, ultimately became just another product in the youth marketplace.

It was the Californians, of course, who first gave surfing the self-consciousness necessary for it to become marketable by introducing the element of "style" to the sport – both in and out of the water.

While postwar America basked in smug suburban bliss and prosperity, the few surfers of the day were already tooling up and down Pacific Coast Highway, shooting the curl from San Onofre to Malibu. Hawaii was still a truly exotic adventure, and as early as the 1940s, surfers visiting the islands for fabulous waves and tropical warmth adopted much of the local cultural style of surfing: an emphasis on physical conditioning and dexterity, along with a laidback attitude, aloha shirts, thongs on their feet, and trunks made loose and comfortable to prevent chafing while astride their boards.

The late 40s and early 50s were a time of discovery for Californian surfers – discovery of what the Golden State's postwar affluence and freedom

Cited as being futurists by some commentators, many surfers have made a leisure pursuit the focal point of their lives. The attraction to the sport often lasts a lifetime.

really had to offer young daredevils in search of fun. There were miles of unspoiled beaches, sea life in great abundance, an almost ideal climate. Taking cues from the Hawaiian surfing experience, Californian surfers of the time began to construct a way of life around their chosen leisure activity. Palm-frond "palapas" similar to those at Waikiki appeared on California beaches. After-surf barbecues and campouts, if not quite luaus, were still not uncommon when a group of surfer guys and girls got together on the weekend. They were in many ways an elite group, and not at all in sync with the prevailing social mood of conformity, family and the Protestant work ethic. But they were still too small a group to be stereotyped and labeled. To be a surfer back then was to be an athlete of more-than-average strength and commitment. Some of the most proficient were lifeguards. The sport was just too difficult and strenuous to gain mass acceptance. But all that was about to change.

Fiberglass brought the first clue that technology could improve the surfer's lot. This "high-tech" material was developed for its high strength-to-weight ratio, a key attribute for components to be used in flying machines. When soaked with

epoxy or isothalic resins, properly catalyzed and allowed to "set" in warm sunlight, fiberglass became a resilient, strong and impervious outer covering for surfboards. As the 40s drew to a close, the best boards were shaped from balsa and red-wood laminates, although some designers were still working with boards rib-constructed from hollow plywood, and polystyrene foam was also being added to the mix of materials in experimental "sandwich-construction" hollow plywood craft.

These wooden hybrids were already lighter than their more traditional, Hawaiian-style predecessors, but balsa tended to soak up sea water like a sponge when damaged, and the hollow boards were more suited for paddling races and lifeguard rescues than riding waves with any kind of real technique. But surfers wanted to be able to turn their boards, accelerate to beat breaking sections of wave, and, most of all, they wanted to be able to ride with flair and style.

At first the shorter, lighter boards met with

Bill Barnfield, surfboard-shaper. The method for producing polyurethane foam and fiberglass boards has changed little from their first appearance in the late 1950s.

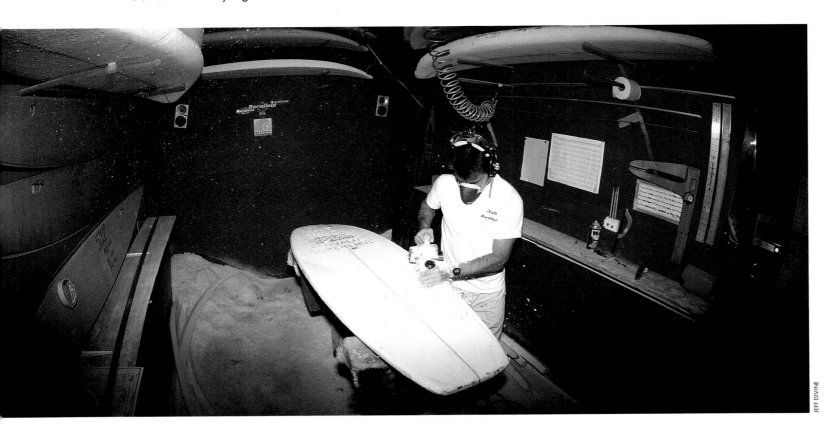

200

some resistance from the "old school" surfers, who saw them as good only for beginners or women, and not suitable for real men. But by 1956 the "Malibu" surfboards – nine feet six inches (2.8 meters) long, constructed of fiberglassed balsa and weighing 25–30 pounds (11–13 kilograms) – were considered state of the art, and made their international debut at the "Surf Olympics" held at Bells Beach in Victoria, Australia.

Balsa wood was always in short supply and subject to rot, imperfections and varying weight. Sections had to be hand-picked, glued and clamped together to form a "blank" big enough for a surfboard, then shaped into the desired design. It was a time-consuming and arduous process. Polyurethane foam provided a solution. A hard but light substance valued by the aerospace industry for its electromagnetic insulating properties, polyurethane foam could also be shaped, just like wood, with carpenters' tools. In addition to being easier to work with than wood, the foam could be manufactured to be less dense and therefore lighter, and was ideal for use with fiberglass and resin. In 1957 Dave Sweet began producing handcrafted foam-and-fiberglass boards in Santa Monica, California, in a manner that has changed little to this day, and other pioneers quickly followed suit. Wooden boards were finished.

Meanwhile, up in Malibu, the surfing scene at the beach was attracting attention from Hollywood moguls with a handle on popular culture and the mood of the times.

Perhaps it was simply Malibu's proximity to the entertainment industry center that made the ensuing love/hate relationship inevitable. Perhaps it was the fact that many actors, screenwriters and producers lived in the beachside community that made surfing a topic that would find its way into their work. Perhaps it was simply that the surfers at Malibu were such a colorful, fascinating and eccentric bunch that their lives made a natural subject for the fantasy factory of film.

Indeed, the Hollywood connection to surfing had already been established for quite some time. Duke Kahanamoku, the "father of modern surf-

Left: A great Australian surfer and surfboard designer — Simon Anderson. Right: Allan Byrne, master surfboard-shaper.

201

ing," had appeared in several Hollywood films over the years. Californian surf pioneer Tom Blake, probably the first surfer to ride Malibu's fabulous waves back in 1926, parlayed his prowess as a waterman and adventurer into a role as stand-in for Clark Gable in the 1940 movie *The Trial of '98*. Johnny "Tarzan" Weissmuller was a regular surfer at Malibu between screen parts.

But this was small stuff compared to what Hollywood was about to dish up. When Frederick Kohner wrote a novel based on stories he'd heard his daughter Kathy tell about the beach scene at Malibu in the summer of 1956, the stage was set for surfing's Hollywood explosion.

Kathy Kohner, it so happened, had been hanging out with a rather extraordinary bunch of surfers in the days when Dad was cooking up his potboiler. Among them were Mickey Dora, Terry "Tubesteak" Tracey, and Billy Al Bengston, later to become an internationally known artist, but in those days called "Moondoggie." It was Tubesteak who first gave Kathy her own nickname. She was a cute, five-foot-tall (152-centimeter) teen, little bigger than a "girl-midget," so Tubesteak dubbed her "Gidget." The movie based (very loosely) on her stories hit the screen in 1959, and nothing about surfing would ever be the same again.

In many ways, the surfers of the 50s had been too cool for their own good. True renaissance men, they had been athletes, adventurers, hedonists and inventors. They'd developed their own style of

Based on the summertime stories of Kathy Kohner, and starring Sandra Dee and James Darren, **Gidget** *(1959) spawned numerous sequels and look-alikes.*

202

dress and their own way of life. They even had their own way of talking. This was actually more the result of a language that had to be invented to describe epic rides, as there were no linguistic precedents for "hotdogging," or "wiping out," and great rides *had* to be talked over and over.

Nevertheless, having their own vernacular gave surfers an even greater aura of mystique. They were also a uniformly macho bunch. So, in retrospect, it was ironic that the tattletales of a girl who'd infiltrated their arcane world brought an end to their age of innocence.

Not that most surfers seemed to mind very much at the time. Surfers were hired as movie extras, as Sandra Dee and James Darren captured the imagination of American teens with *Gidget*, and sequels and knockoffs went into production. Gidget herself responded more like a genuine surfer and got on a plane for the islands in *Gidget Goes Hawaiian* (1961), but by 1963 *Beach Party* hit the screens with Frankie Avalon and Annette Funicello pouring it on about how much fun, how much heartache, and how much hype could go into growing up at the beach in California. By the time Hollywood got around to *How to Stuff a Wild Bikini* (65), it all had very little to do with what surfers had been about just five years before.

As Hollywood happily churned out more such stereotypical adolescent melodrama – *Gidget Goes to Rome* (63), *Muscle Beach Party* (64),

Beach Blanket Bingo (65) to name but a few – another marketing angle emerged from the recording industry. Dick Dale and the Deltones, for example, were packing houses as early as 1961, and Dale went so far as to call himself "King of the Surf Guitar." His cascading licks on the Fender were his rock 'n' roll rendition, he said, of waves breaking over the surfer's back as he rode inside the tube. All of a sudden there was a phenomenon called "surf music" and, riding the crest of success, bands like the Beach Boys, Ventures, Surfaris and Jan & Dean had teenagers flocking to sock hops to do "the surfer stomp."

The packaging of surfing by the entertainment industry had long-lasting implications for the sport. The most obvious, and most enduring, was the stereotype of surfers as being rather empty-headed malingerers with a penchant for parties and the daughters of the middle classes. It was a fine line between being a surfer and being a "beach bum" in the early 60s, but by the middle of the decade

there was little collective doubt that surfers were on the more unsavory side of the line.

Still, there was no doubt that genuine surf fever was sweeping America and, indeed, the world. The newly modern surf industry in California was ready to cater to an unprecedented demand for boards. As beach movies prospered at the box office and surf music topped the charts, surfboard shops proliferated, and cottage-industry seamstresses who'd sewed trunks for the neighborhood boys became overnight sportswear magnates.

While there's no denying surfing was the teen fad of 1963–65, plenty of those who took up surfing because it was the happening thing soon became genuinely hooked. Once they actually experienced the thrill of riding a wave they found personal rewards that exceeded all their expectations. To begin with, there was the natural high of being physically fit – an immediate hidden benefit. Next came the catharsis of simply surviving. As Dr Scott Jenkins of Scripps Institution of Oceanography so aptly says: "When you paddle out, you enter the food chain." As young surfers learned to conquer fear – of sharks or fish-killing closeouts – they found it felt good, built character and self-esteem, and made the usual adolescent trials and tribulations seem insignificant by comparison. Behind all the hype of Hollywood's portrayal of the beach scene was a very real youth-culture phenomenon, and when real surfers went to a "surf movie" it was for a very different experience from the Hollywood version.

The genuine surf movie had its origins in the simple camaraderie of the sport's early days. What could be more fun, after all, than being able to film yourself and a few buddies going surfing, then reliving the experience in the den or clubhouse? As early as the 30s and 40s, surfers had been keen to see themselves or others riding great waves in California or Hawaii, although these early efforts were little more than the stuff of home movies. Serious surf film-making began 10 years later with Bud Browne, and by the end of the 50s this pioneer had a string of titles to his credit, including *The Big Surf*, *Hawaiian Surfing Memories* and *Trek to Makaha*. Browne even pioneered water cinematography during these years, putting his 16 mm movie camera inside a waterproof rubber bag to get those shark's-eye views of surfers, up close and personal, caught in the act.

There was a flurry of activity on the surf-movie scene at this time. Bruce Brown (no relation to Bud Browne) wowed surf-stoked audiences with movies like *Slippery When Wet* (59) in a way that presaged his future role as the maker of the most influential surf movie of all time – *Endless Summer*. John Severson had helped raise the standard of surf movies in 1958 with *Surf Safari*, but two years later released *Surf Fever*, along with a promotional brochure that would prove so popular that it quickly developed into *Surfer* magazine, the Severson periodical that became known as "the bible" of the emerging subculture. Meanwhile, surfers gathered in large, noisy, exuberant crowds at surf-movie shows in theaters, clubhouses and high-school auditoriums.

Another movie that caught the mood of surfing in 64 was the Hollywood release *Ride the Wild Surf*. This was the first movie to show lots of huge waves being ridden in glorious 35 mm, big-screen images. And to surfers everywhere the location footage of surf action on Oahu's north shore was all the more compelling because the primary surfers/stand-ins dueling it out at Sunset Beach and Waimea Bay were none other than Greg Noll and Mickey Dora, wave riders of legendary status in the sport. Aside from the big-wave drama, however,

204

the movie signaled another cue to surfing's emerging culture. So they could be easily differentiated, Dora wore red-and-yellow paneled surf trunks, while Noll wore his own black-and-white hooped trunks: the custom-made "icon" board shorts of "The Bull." The movie had hit on another important aspect of the growing sport by alluding to surfers' obsession with personal style.

The concept of style was all-consuming – from the way a surfer held his hands while trimming across a walled-up wave, the color of the panels and stripes on his surfboard, and the way its wooden stringer was laminated (T-band, or reverse T-band? *That* was the question), to the shorts and tee-shirts he would wear.

In fact, by the mid-60s, surf fashion was already well established. What had begun with simple tee-shirts adorned with a surfboard-maker's decal, had become "lifestyle apparel," where the label was often more important than the look. Hang Ten was the first on the scene in 1961, and even today, when toes-over-the-nose is no longer a state-of-the-art surfing maneuver (most grom-

mets probably don't even know what the two little feet signify), the Hang Ten logo is licensed to over 100 manufacturers in 45 countries around the world.

For those who were already out in the early 60s lineup, there was an incredible wave of success to be ridden. Surf wear would become a multi-million-dollar-a-year enterprise going on all over the globe. In the meantime, fortunes were made almost overnight, not only in clothing, but in hard goods, raw materials for boards, and spinoffs like skateboarding – "sidewalk surfing" as it was called, which in turn became the infatuation of surfers, and the landlocked masses who wanted to be surfers.

With growing numbers of participants and a buoyant economy, surfing and the surfing industry boomed. But surfers became very aware of what was real and what was fake, and impostors and "wannabes" were quickly dismissed as "hodads." Similarly, they were equally discerning about the products they bought, and were able to smell a scam or rip-off being perpetrated by outsiders who thought there was a quick buck to be made. Meanwhile, board makers discovered the influence they could exert with surf teams. The hottest riders were sponsored, usually with free equipment and travel. Some even found jobs as shapers, glassers and shop managers. Hard-core surfers all, they could hardly believe their luck – they were being paid for living the life they loved. Invariably, they were the best performers of the day.

But not everyone in the sport was totally enamored with surfing's "progress," and the surfing community splintered – into "soul surfers," who rejected all the commercialization, competition and hype, and the rest: supporters of growth, development of surfing as a true "sport," and making a living out of a lifestyle.

As American society in general pulled itself apart over issues like the Vietnam War, civil rights, psychedelic drugs and the sexual revolution, surfing underwent a startling metamorphosis of its own; turning inward on itself, rejecting society's view of it, reverting, as it were, to the purity of its roots. In the water, style was defined as flowing with the wave . . . of becoming one with it. There was much debate about whether surfing was a sport or an art. For those who subscribed to the latter point of view, and they were many, surfing took on an aura of mysticism, and riding waves was described as a Zen experience.

On land, surfing's clean-cut image took enough knocks to bring back the stereotype of the beach bum. But the soul surfers delighted in being right in sync with the rebellious times – they were even applauded by counter-cultural gurus like Timothy Leary and Herbert Marcuse, who cited surfers as being futurists; the first people to make a leisure pursuit the focal point of their lives.

Many surfers, having reached their mid-twenties and embarked upon marriage and career, gave up the sport at this time. But a lot of others took a hippie detour by turning on, tuning out and dropping in — on as many waves as they could, in places as remote as they could find, paying for it however they could, with as little effort as possible.

But far from being a death knell for surfing, this troublesome sea change turned into its rebirth. As it happened, and perhaps even because of it, a major advance in equipment once again provided the impetus. When the shortboard revolution of 1968–70 took place, there were suddenly myriad performance barriers to be torn down as surfers discovered radical, tight-arc maneuvers and new approaches to wave riding, especially in and around the curl. Those on the cutting edge at the time went on to redefine what was possible, and once again surfing developed a whole new style.

Surfing will no doubt continue to change and evolve. In fact, for a surfer, the concept of constant change is an essential element. Learning from the ebb and flow of tides, the effects of wind upon the water, the swells that build and die, surfers live with the rhythm of change every day. Only one element stays the same: then as now, surfing is a whole lot of fun.

205

Above: **A** *board, a wave and somewhere to sleep: all the self-sufficient surfer needs.* **Below**: *Grommets and pros the world over say the same thing: surfing is a whole lot of fun.*

SUBCULTURE

NICK CARROLL

SKATEBOARDS

One day in 1962 a bunch of kids was playing around outside a surf shop in California. The surf was flat and they were bored. So they got hold of an old boxcar-style scooter chassis and began running it up and down the street, standing on it like it was a surfboard. And so an astonishing craze, sport, cult pursuit and lifestyle was born.

Skateboarders – ''skateheads'' – were once just surfers in a flat spell. Now they carry the cachet of their very own subculture. In many ways this is a strong reflection of how surfing once was, back in those zany, rebellious days of the 60s.

Skate kids today are street-loving kids who wear street-hip clothes, listen to skate-thrash bands that sound like 70s punk cranked up to twice the speed, and talk about ''slams,'' ''killer airs,'' ''ollies'' and ''totally gnarly ramps.'' There are millions of them, from the mean streets of east LA to urban Tokyo and gritty London parks. And just as surely as surf music, talk and clothes turned groovy, skate stuff – with its outrageous graphics and tough-kid appeal – is heading in the same direction.

The great invention back in 62 kicked off a sudden overwhelming charge of interest in the sport, with big surf manufacturers gearing up to produce boards and even a song – ''Sidewalk Surfin' '' – which put skateboarding in its spot as a surfer's backup weapon. The interest didn't last. Right until the 1980s, skating tended to run in boom–bust cycles. A company would come out with a new kind of skate gear, like the polyurethane wheels that appeared in the early 70s. Kids would go bananas and everyone would need a skateboard. But without the backing of something more than the fly-by-night business people who tried cashing in with cheap gear, the fad would fade as soon as it started.

It was the hard-core skaters, the guys and girls who did it as an end, rather than an occupation for flat surf spells, who dragged skating into the 80s with bigger, wider boards (''decks''), wide

No longer just something for surfers to do in a flat spell, skateboarding today carries the cachet of its very own subculture.

MARTIN TULLEMANS

wheels and trucks and, most important, a set of skating moves quite distinct from the turns, trims and stalls of a surfer. Skate parks and a vast potential market made the USA a logical place for the start of a skate renaissance.

Then came Stacy Peralta and his Bones Brigade.

Peralta, a smart Californian dude who'd made it as a big-name skater in the 70s, started a skate-gear company and pulled together a team of high-powered performers to promote it. The Bones Brigade, including world champions Tony Hawk and Steve Caballero, took the New Skating to the world via a series of videos designed to blow the minds of grommets everywhere.

Now there are ramps scattered across the parks and backyards of practically the whole Western world. Unlike surfers, skaters don't need to live near the ocean, and their sport is as easily performed on an indoor ramp or city street. This accessibility should keep skate kids going for a long, long time.

SAILBOARDS

Sailboarding looks like it should be an outcrop of surfboard riding. Many tales tracing its origins make this seem like a rational idea, too. For instance, in the early 30s photographers could capture images of young men lying on boards in the waters of Waikiki, using a braced sail to drift about in the sun and have a great old time. The famed surfboard designer of the time, Tom Blake, actually set a sail on one of his long, hollow boards and took it for a run off Diamond Head, only to be forced to paddle back when he discovered he couldn't turn around and sail. Later Blake got it together enough to have races across Waikiki on his mini-yachts, using a rudder to steer.

Sailboarding exists very much on its own. The brilliant, esoteric area of wavesailing is just a branch of a sport practised more in the lakes and stillwater seas of Europe than in the wild oceans off Australia and Hawaii, although both those countries can claim more than their share of champions.

Sailboarding owes its key element to a couple of Californian engineers called Hoyle Schweitzer and Jim Drake, who weren't interested in surfing at all. They were interested in the universal joint.

The joint, which allows the mast and sail on modern sailboards to revolve, twist and generally do whatever the sailboarder wants it to do, was invented by Schweitzer and Drake in 1969, and promptly copied by dozens of manufacturers worldwide. Hoyle Schweitzer was enraged, beginning a series of exhausting court actions that eventually netted him patents and around $34 million in royalties. By the time he'd finished 15 years later, sailboarding looked nothing like it had when he'd kicked it off.

First, in countries like Holland and Germany, where surfing had never even been considered, sailboarding had found

Although sailboarding looks like it should be an offshoot of surfing, the exchange of innovative design features between the sports has been a two-way process.

its natural market. Here was something that young, trendy Europeans could do with ease, something that was already developing an international groove.

Second, a band of surf nuts called Pat Love, Larry Stanley and Mike Horgan had headed off to Hawaii and taken the sailboarding rig into the surf. They set up a shop at Kailua on the island of Oahu and taught a nine-year-old kid who'd been into catamarans, Robbie Naish, how to boardsail. Pretty soon Robbie was the best thing to step on to the rig. He was followed out into the waves off Kailua and Diamond Head by Mike Waltze, Malte Simmer and Matt Schweitzer – that's right, Hoyle's son.

Although sailboarding's origins aren't strictly surf-oriented, the surf adventures of Naish and the crew inspired

surfsailing around the world among both regular sailors and surfers. Sailboarding and surfing go well together for a number of reasons, a major one being that the howling winds needed for a good sailing session normally rule out good surfing conditions. Surfers and sailboarders have been able to learn from each other's equipment, with design basics like vee and tri-fins going into the early surf-sailboards and trickier stuff like asymmetrics and slot-fins coming back the other way.

SURF MOVIES

In 1964 a laconic American character who'd just spent a couple of years roaming the world with a movie camera finally put out his flick. The American,

Bruce Brown, had taken two surfers named Mike Hynson and Robert August to places like Africa, Australia, Tahiti and Hawaii. The idea was to get some waves and have as good a time as possible. Brown had the film edited and put down a simple music and narration soundtrack. But his true act of genius came with the name: *Endless Summer*.

There'd been surf movies before this. There'd even been bizarre Hollywood muscle-beach movies, trying to glitz surfing into a million-dollar hayride. *Endless Summer* did something hardly any of the other flicks had approached: it explained surfing and surfers to themselves. The romance of chasing perfect waves around the planet, never being caught by the mundaneness of everyday life, was exactly why the surfers of the 60s had taken up their sport.

The fact that the movie ended up grossing millions tells us something of just how important surf flicks have been to their audiences. In the 1960s they were one of the few reasons a bunch of surfers would gather in public off the beach. Few of the movies were any good, either in film quality or structure, but that was hardly the point. Old-time cinema owners who showed such movies as *Pacific Vibrations*, *High on a Cool Wave* and *Evolution* can tell horrifying tales of the surf kids howling with glee and throwing everything from ice cream to beer cans as they rolled in the aisles – literally, that is. Movie nights in Huntington Beach, California, and Avalon Theater on Sydney's north side were legendary.

But the movies weren't just an excuse to go animal. In the days before the pro tour, they were the only chance a surfer had to see the greats of the sport in action. They were *communication* – first between Hawaii and California, then between California and Australia, then all over the world. Champion Australian surfer of the 60s Peter Drouyn can recall it clearly: ''We all waited for those movies! We waited and waited with bated breath for the next one. It was like the next chapter of a novel. When it

JOHN WITZIG

SURF FILM

In Person
BRUCE BROWN
Showing and narrating
his latest film

"Barefoot Adventure"

PRESENTED BY
SURFING PROMOTIONS
AT
CREMORNE ORPHEUM
ON
FRI. 5th JANUARY
8 p.m.   BOOK NOW !

FULL COLOR
in
HAWAII & CALIFORNIA

Original
musical score
composed and
performed
by
BUD
SHANK
with
Bob Cooper
Carmell Jones
Dennis Budimir
Gary Peacock
and
Shelly Manne

... "A Ring-A-Ding Thriller!"—Charles Champlin, TIME Magazine

JOHN WITZIG

The Endless Summer

finally came we were all nervous, pulling holes in seats and hooting. It was that sort of scene."

Endless Summer set some sort of standard for the surf movie, and into the 70s the quality steadily climbed, peaking with the 1978 release *Free Ride*, which did for pro surfing what Brown's movie did for surfing's romantic face. But as surfing moved into the 1980s, the surfing magazines stepped up their acts and grommets could watch Tom Curren, Tom Carroll and Mark Occhilupo in a pro contest near them. The surfing movie drooped. Theaters weren't interested, the veteran film-makers were growing older and their protégés saw little point in spending years of work on something that, if they were lucky, might break even. Recently, though, financial backing by the big surf companies has seen a revival of the movie in video form, with tapes like *Wave Warriors*, *All Down the Line* and *Gripping Stuff* tackling surfing 90s style.

THE ENVIRONMENT

In the early 1960s, when a development company decided it had to tag a boat harbor on to a section of southern Californian coast, a famous surf spot named Dana Point was lost forever. Arguably, this was the first serious thing to happen in surfing. It focused the minds of surfers on to an issue that was to turn into the mushroom cloud of the 1990s: the environment.

Back in the 60s "environment" was one of those words associated with child psychology or a raving hippie minority. The idea that any sort of development should be slowed or halted out of concern for the natural world was something that smacked of communism, or worse. But surfers were touching the natural world at a basic level unknown in other sports, where "nature" was the grass on the football field or the rough on the golf course. Playing in the ocean, traveling the coastline without much money in search of clean waves, made surfers environmentalists almost by default.

Their concerns took different shapes in different parts of the world. In Australia coastal sandmining was the surfers' issue. A magazine called *Tracks* was founded in 1970, its almost exclusive intention being to fight the mining that was sucking the life out of the dreamlike beaches of northern New South Wales. *Tracks*-inspired or not, the sandminers were stopped soon afterwards, but the magazine kept on while surfers and surfing drifted into hippiedom, running long articles about healthy eating, self-sufficiency and even a series on how to build a house for almost nothing. Surfing, youth and campaigns like Greenpeace's Save the Whales became thoroughly intertwined.

By the 80s surfers had successfully helped to confront the ocean pollution problem in Australian cities, earning

banner newspaper headlines in the process. For many Australians, one of the lasting impressions of that decade will be the picture of anti-nuclear activist Ian Cohen clinging to the bow of a US nuclear-powered warship in Sydney Harbor, balanced on his surfboard.

In America, surfers had different battles to fight, and chose different weapons. They used organization. Organization was the only way to deal with the myriad threats to the US surfing population, from over-eager developers to missile defense installations to simple sewage overflow. In response to that, a group called the Surfrider Foundation was pulled together in 1984 by older surfers who'd carved out names and positions for themselves in both business and the science of environment. The foundation – or "Surfrider," as they prefer – takes up the cause of its 2700 lay and two dozen corporate members in courtrooms, councils and committees, against some of the most powerful business interests in the nation. To date they have scored victories for surfers in San Diego, Orange County and Santa Barbara, and next on the list is the most ambitious environment proposal of all – artificial reefs. The idea: don't just save surf, make more of it.

B*eginning in the* 1980s*, surfers joined forces with other beachgoers and concerned citizens to confront the problem of ocean pollution in Australian cities.*

MARTIN TULLEMANS

The Beach Boys were riding the crest of the surf-music wave when this photo was taken in 1964.

apocalyptic messengers. Several of the Boys turned to booze and worse, with the genius Brian Wilson being surrounded by ugly hangers-on who sucked him dry and sent him into psychiatric care. Brian's analyst eventually tempted him back into songwriting and producing in 1976, and the band came back on the charts for a while. But – as if to prove that the simple fun of the 60s were long gone – Dennis drowned in a drunken boating accident in 1983. The Beach Boys were inducted into the Rock'n'Roll Hall of Fame in 1988.

THE BEACH BOYS

If one thing was more effective than Hollywood beach-party celluloid at spreading the surfing word, it was surf music. And without doubt, the biggest thing in surf music was the Beach Boys.

The Boys – Brian, Carl and Dennis Wilson, Mike Love and Al Jardine – weren't the originators of surf sound. That honor might go to the left-handed guitar player Dick Dale, whose sliding Stratocaster sound was an innovative attempt to capture surfing with an instrument. The Beach Boys tried for more. They wanted to put it into words: not just surfing, but girls, cars, free-and-easy days, the whole Californian youth lifestyle of the 60s wrapped up in one attractive harmonic parcel.

The Boys came out of the Los Angeles suburb of Hawthorne, first as Carl and the Passions, then Kenny and the Cadets. Candix, their first record label, suggested the Beach Boys as a tricky title. Dennis was the surfer of the group, but the musical brain was Brian Wilson, who once wrote the first chord progressions for *Surfin' USA* in a school music class and was reprimanded by the teacher for not working on "melody." In 1961 Wilson and his brothers and their buddies took their chords, their harmonies and their clean-cut goodness to the American

public and knocked 'em dead.

The Beach Boys did songs like *Barbara Anne* and *Surfin' Safari*, the Chantays did *Pipeline*, and surf music went off the deep end. In five years hundreds of surf songs, instrumentals and "stomps" were recorded across the globe. Some of the names – both bands and songs – were hysterical. Tom and Jerry's *Surfin' Hootenanny*; Surf Teens' *Surf Mania*; Spinners' *Party – My Pad After Surfin'*. The craze spread to Australia, where Little Pattie's Maroubra Surf Stomps were legendary.

How many of these musicians surfed? Does it matter? Surfing hit a glamor peak in the days of early 60s surf music, a peak it may never again attain. The Beach Boys were riding not just the wave of a fabulous sport, but a surge of youth culture that in the next decade would change the world faster than ever before. They did weepies (*Surfer Girl*, 1963) and zanies (*Fun, Fun, Fun*, 1964) with equal brilliance, and in 1966 hit the heights with *Good Vibrations* – perhaps the best-known of all surf tunes, and a number one worldwide.

It did not last. With the coming of flower power, surf music vanished as swiftly as it was created, replaced by the Doors, Jimi Hendrix (who hung out with surfers on Maui making *Rainbow Bridge*), the Beatles and other

SURF WAGONS

In the beginning, there was the woody. Then came the convertible, the Kombi, the pickup and the Porsche. Today it might be anything from a family wagon to an airplane. The kinds of car surfers have used to get to and from waves, parties, countries and surfboard factories is a wonderful reflection on the state of the subculture.

In the postwar years, when America took the automobile in a feverish embrace, the key was to get a car – somehow. Money didn't exist, but surfers needed vehicles that would take their surfboards first and them second. A famous early surf car was Bob Simmons's Model A Ford, the back end surgically removed for easy board insertion. Even better were the cheap wood-paneled wagons built by Ford and British BMG as small working vehicles in the 1950s: you could stuff your boards in the back and climb in with 'em, the driver and a couple of others in front. Thus was born the day of the "woody," and the "little deuce coupé" two-seater of Beach Boys legend.

As surfers turned counter-cultural in the early 70s, they began looking for vehicles in which to "drop out." To drop out successfully, you needed a bigger car than a woody. You needed a portable

LEROY GRANNIS

house, something big enough for your partner, your Afghan hound, your surfboard, your bed and your copy of *Jonathan Livingston Seagull*. For American surfers this might mean a pickup with built back, or a souped-up family monster wagon, even an old bus. For Australians it might mean the terrifying panel van, a beast of a car. It was designed for tradespeople and had an outsize rear end strapped on to a standard wagon body. But for surfers all over the world, this was the era of the Kombi: a squared-off creature from Germany with sliding side doors, a cranky engine, a mixed-up gearbox and a deep desire to drink more fuel than it deserved. For all its oddball faults, the Kombi was a sturdy animal that crashed through bushes as well as the next car and carried any load with the same puttering relentlessness.

The Kombis kept going for so long – some of them are still in service in the 90s – that surfing's sudden burst of wealth caught them almost by surprise. A perfect illustration of this was when in 1981 world champ Mark Richards returned home from a particularly

successful session on tour with about $40,000 in his pocket. Waiting at his Newcastle, New South Wales, house was his faithful Kombi. But on the way home from the airport MR passed a Porsche salesroom. Unable to help himself, the champ raced in, slapped down the money and set off home in a shining

Built by Ford and BMG in the 1950s, the ''woody'' became synonymous with traveling surfer-style.

silver 911 that made the pages of every surfing magazine on earth.

This was a new era – an era for flaunting it, if you had it. Tom Carroll picked up an Alfa, Damien Hardman a sports Integra, and the Hawaiian highways echoed to the sound of giant-tired pickups with chrome hanging from every angle. And when *Surfing* magazine editor Bill Sharp appeared in his own publication driving a red Ferrari with the numberplate INDTUBE, the trend was firmly set. Surfing was hip.

JEFF DIVINE

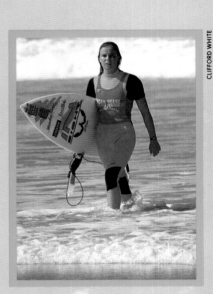

Surfriders

All *great surfers have one
thing in common — beautiful
control in outrageous
situations. Here Tom Curren
plays it cool beneath Pipeline's
furious embrace.*
Inset: Wendy Botha.

Wendy Botha

GARY DUNNE

First, in 1987, there was a South African by the name of Wendy Botha who became the women's world professional surfing champion. Then two years later there was an Australian by the name of Wendy Botha who became the women's world professional surfing champion.

Those title wins were not by two people who uncannily shared the same name. They were achieved by the same person – an articulate, friendly young woman with a remarkable talent for riding waves.

She learnt to surf on the waves that broke on the reefs, beaches and points around her home town of East London, a few hundred miles south of Durban on South Africa's Indian Ocean coast.

As a 13-year-old, male school friends introduced Wendy to the surfboards and waves that now dominate her life. As the only girl in town who surfed, it was inevitable that she was to be strongly influenced in her approach to surfing by the boys who'd led her into the waves. Within two years Botha won her first South African national title.

214

TONY NOLAN

Botha's pursuit of improvement in her surfing drove her into the men's competitive ranks. It was a move she acknowledges as a major contribution to the development of her surfing, and one which led to the establishment of her links with Australia. In 1982 Bill Bolman (an Australian who was then contest director of the famed Stubbies Classic on Queensland's Gold Coast) was in Africa and saw Botha competing against the men at a contest at Jeffreys Bay. He recognized the already obvious skill and invited Botha to compete in the next Stubbies Classic. She accepted and so began her extraordinary climb to the top of the international professional ranks. In 1983, as a 17-year-old amateur with three African titles to her credit, Botha went to Australia and finished second to a young Australian woman who'd finished runner-up in the world title the previous season – Pam Burridge.

In 1985 Botha went to Australia for an eight-month stay and won her first two professional events – the BHP Steel International and the Stubbies Classic, but inconsistent results in the other events saw her end the year ranked seventh in the world.

In the 1986 season, despite winning only one event – the Stubbies Classic, again – Botha moved up the world rankings to fifth. In 1987 Botha realized her potential for the first time, winning the first three contests and finishing second in another to secure her first world title. That victory made Botha the first non-American world champion in the 11-year history of women's professional surfing.

In 1988, having moved to Australia to be coached by former male professional Greg Day, Botha dropped down the world rankings to third; even though she won more events (three) than any of her rivals.

But if 1988 was a disappointment for Botha, 1989 was the ultimate comeback. She devastated her rivals, winning seven of the 12 events, including four of the first five, to become only the second surfer in either professional division to regain a world title.

Her efforts literally forced the rewriting of the

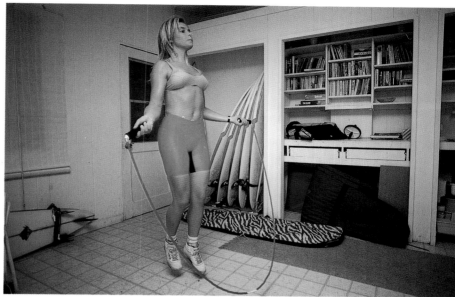

TED GRAMBEAU

Botha is relentlessly fit. **Above**: *Working out in Hawaii.* **Opposite**: *Using her strength to slam the board high on a Sydney beachbreak.*

Association of Surfing Professionals' record books. By winning more than US$44,000, Botha lifted herself to the top of the single season and career prize money lists, and the seven wins meant she joined four-time world champion Frieda Zamba at the top of the career victories list, with 15 wins. And she'd done some of it as an Australian, having been naturalized in October of that year.

Botha's motivation to leave her family, childhood friends and the country of her birth to become an Australian was fairly simple. In the 13-year history of women's professional surfing to the end of 1989, there'd never been a women's pro event in South Africa. As Botha has said: "Being a professional female surfer in South Africa was like being a professional snow skier and living in a desert."

Botha's surfing style is one of grace and poise, combined with power and aggression. Those characteristics of her surfing are the product of an often stated desire and determination to "surf like men, or better than men." That style has earned her, particularly, and women's surfing generally, a greater degree of respect than ever before from the harshest critics of women's surfing – their male counterparts.

Tom Carroll

JOHN ELLISS

TED GRAMBEAU

Tom Carroll's backside assault, along with his calm and friendly nature, have made him a hero to thousands of grommets worldwide. **Spread**: *Tom places one of those surgical turns into a Log Cabins peeler.* **Left**: *A thoughtful character.*

A few surfers have left their mark on surfing but the 1980s belonged to Tom Carroll. Competitively and in pure performance he is the most influential surfer of the past decade, and when 1990 rolled around he had garnered a reputation as the best all-round surfer in the world.

Carroll has been a dominant figure in surfing since the late 70s. First as the up-and-coming grommet, then as the one-most-likely-to. He was heir apparent to Mark Richards and fulfilled the inevitable when he won back-to-back world titles in 1983 and 1984.

Tom Carroll has been competing full-time in the world professional circuit since 1982 and has finished in the top five every year. He has influenced surfing in many ways. He emerged from a fiercely competitive pack of young surfers at Newport Beach on Sydney's north side. In the late 70s and early 80s this group produced a number of Australian champions and a string of professional surfers.

In 1982 Carroll took on Peter Colbert as his manager, the first full-time manager in professional surfing. Colbert managed Carroll's business and travel affairs, allowing Tom to concentrate on his surfing. The partnership with Colbert lasted seven years and during that time Carroll was one of the few surfers to attract endorsement from outside the surfing industry and was the first surfer to sign a million-dollar contract.

As Carroll's earnings grew, similar contracts began to filter through the professional ranks to the point where most surfers seeded in the top 30 earn a good living.

Carroll is also responsible for the introduction of serious training to pro surfing. He has a close understanding of his body, with diet and mental preparation being major factors in his success. Carroll has shown that a surfer can improve once he's past 25 and at the end of 1989 he was surfing better than when he won his world titles. Other surfers have witnessed this and today serious training and attention to diet are a part of every top competitor's regimen.

Throughout his career Tom has received wide

JEFF DIVINE

coverage in the Australian media and he is one of the best-known sportsmen in the country. An intelligent and well-read man, Carroll sometimes has trouble articulating his thoughts, something that has improved with experience but which attracted criticism in the early part of his career.

In 1985 he shocked the surfing world and the Australian public when he announced his decision to boycott the South African leg of the pro tour. This was a personal stand against apartheid but his failure to clearly state his motive led to the decision being misunderstood by many and resulted in much personal anguish for Tom.

"It was disheartening to see people think and say and write that my stand against apartheid was superficial. My sole aim was to express concern after touring South Africa four times. When you're in South Africa as a surfer and a white man it's so easy to live like a king and ignore what's going on – some people are affected by a situation, others aren't. It's an ugly system and all I could see was there'd been no real attempt to improve the situation."

While Tom's competitive nature has always been an important factor in his motivation to improve, it is the actual wave riding that is paramount. His surfing, more than anything, will be his legacy to the sport. He has pushed surfing in all conditions to unforeseen levels. He has successfully melded the pure ethics of surfing – style, speed and power – with the rigid demands of competition. He has developed into a true big-wave master, dominating the last few seasons in Hawaii and earning the unrivaled respect of his peers.

"Surfing should be stylish, strong, powerful

and smooth. The wave should be used with your own style, not something that's contrived. Surfing can't be learnt through a certain routine or technique. Anyone can stand on a surfboard but it's their own personal style which determines whether or not they improve," Tom says. "I just go out and go surfing and ride the wave the way I feel it should be ridden."

All Down the Line, a movie starring Tom and released in 1989, illustrates this perfectly. The sequences filmed in the isolated waves of Indonesia are awe-inspiring. Nick Carroll, Tom's brother, who accompanied him on the trip, said it was a peak of Tom's career. "Riding perfect waves out of nothing but his love for surfing. That's when you see surfing become an art. Surfing is definitely Tom's area of self-expression."

Carroll's concentration, when he chooses to exert it, is absolutely fearsome — even in small foamies, which are not an area he is known to love.

PROFESSIONAL RANKING

1982	3rd	1985	3rd	1988	3rd
1983	1st	1986	2nd	1989	5th
1984	1st	1987	4th		

MAJOR CAREER VICTORIES

1977   Pepsi Pro Junior, Narrabeen, Australia
1978   Australian Junior Championships, Margaret River, Australia
1982   World Cup, Sunset Beach, Hawaii
1983   Coca-Cola Surfabout, Narrabeen, Australia
1984   Marui Pro, Japan
1985   Bells Beach Easter Classic, Australia
1986   Drug Offensive Thriller, Margaret River, Australia
1987   Maui Pipeline Masters, Hawaii
Drug Offensive Thriller, Margaret River, Australia
1988   Hard Rock World Cup, Sunset Beach, Hawaii
1989   BHP Steel International, Newcastle, Australia

PETER SIMONS

PETER BROUILLET

Tom Curren

DEREK HYND

In 1989 Tom Curren was semi-retired, living and surfing around Biarritz, France. He had little left to prove. Yet, eight in every 10 pros still rated him "The Best." Twice world champion, in 1985 and 1986, his form was a cut above. Many said he'd actually improved. In the few small-wave events he entered through the year, his surfing was faster, more precise, than the others. He pulled bigger crowds, threw bigger sprays; he captured the imagination, just like always. His impact was unbe-

lievable. So much so that he is, arguably, the surfer of our time. From the moment he captured the 1980 World Junior Title, the adulation has not let up.

Hailing from Santa Barbara, California, as early as 1979 he was labeled "The Great American Hope" and "America's future world champion." At only 15 years of age, the pressure on Curren to perform was enormous. His cat-like, natural-footed style, honed at famous Rincon Point, carried him to victory in the 1980 World Junior Titles in France. And from then, the promise of things to come changed the way Americans perceived surfers.

There is no way around it — this man, with his cool poise, retiring nature and single-minded competitive skills, is a freak.
Above: Tom Curren slides across Backdoor.

TONY NOLAN

Young, well mannered, quiet, Tom Curren replaced the dirty long-haired dropout as Californian society's perception of the average surfer. The son of legendary Waimea Bay rider Pat Curren, Tom's pro debut was remarkable because he appeared to carry more knowledge into the arena than anyone else, even the three times world champion Mark Richards. It was August 1982, at the inaugural OP Pro. His poise, savvy and wave utilization astounded the best surfers in the world. He was already a threat to their rankings . . . and he hadn't even warmed up. His fifth placing could have been a win, with any more luck. But he won the next event, in Japan, to announce the new era. Within a month of turning pro he had the future by the neck.

In 1983 he won three majors – Australia's Straight Talk Tyres Open, America's OP Pro and Japan's Marui Pro – and also married French girlfriend of three years, Marie Pascale Delanne. If anyone was setting up a career, it was Tom Curren. Tom Carroll and Martin Potter were his new-era rivals, though it was a tender young Mark Occhilupo who clamored to catch him. Occhilupo saw the challenge: "Mate, I was just starting to get good then; but I knew Tommy [Curren] was The Guy, more than anyone realized . . . Tom Carroll was who I admired, but Tommy Curren was the future."

By mid-1984, with a little help from a provocative Occhilupo surfing magazine interview, The Rivalry was born. Over the next two years the

beautiful six- to eight-feet (1.8–2.5-meter) rights, he needed victory to secure his first world title. It was one of the greatest man-on-man heats ever seen. They simply strived for perfection, and found it. Despite being underscored through the first half, Curren took his world title with flawless dump re-entries. For Occhilupo, it was his last great surge. Their paths split.

Even before Curren had won his first world title, the American surf industry was booming in response to his electricity, particularly at the OP Pros. His reticent, even reclusive, demeanor appealed to the market. It was as if he was the shy next-door neighbor who rarely came out to play . . . but when he did! When he surfed, the public thought it was the greatest show on earth, from the nicest guy in town.

Some of Tom's greatest surfing has been done at Bells Beach, Australia, the place where he clinched both his world championships. Above: Tom frightens the daylights out of an innocent Bells section.

Curren–Occhilupo battles elevated the standard so much that any event lucky enough to host one of the encounters was an automatic hit with the public. Curren's performances in winning the 1984 OP Pro, his sponsor's event, and losing in subsequent years to his arch rival, were legendary. The maneuvers he completed in the 1985 and 1986 OP Pros were some of the finest ever witnessed. However, the pinnacle of his talent came at Easter, 1986, at the Rip Curl Bells Beach Pro, in Australia. Against his arch-rival Occhilupo once more, in

The hectic pace of the world tour affected his levels through 1987 and 1988. The motivation was gone. Despite a brilliant finish in the latter year, he retired to his modest villa in Anglet, France, to prepare for family life and surf the fabulous waves at his doorstep. Rumors abounded. Had he really retired? Was it just a feint? Did he want the chance to charge at everybody, from the back marker, in the 1990s? The year 1989 was Martin Potter's year. But on the odd occasion Tom Curren turned up and stole his thunder – in California, France and Hawaii. They were magical moments of games-manship.

There's no way the Curren statement is finished. No way. Chances are, by the time you read this, he'll have mounted the killer comeback.

Barton Lynch

KIRK WILLCOX

He's been called everything from the thinking person's surfer to Mr Consistent, but there is no doubt that Barton Lynch is the most underrated surfer ever to take out a world title.

The scrawny little kid from Manly Beach, Sydney, had a vision of surfing greatness when he was only nine and he doggedly pursued his dream amidst a throng of detractors.

His early dedication brought resentment from his mates because Barton wasn't being one of the boys and going out and getting drunk, acting like the usual Australian adolescent.

One day he turned up on the beach to find the fins kicked off his board and a pair of garden shears stuck in it. "These attacks only served to strengthen my character and increase my desire to achieve," he said later.

After a successful amateur and pro-am career, in 1983 Lynch climbed into the Top 16 at thirteenth place after his second world professional tour. In 1984 he was eighth and in 1985 he was a serious title contender, but finished runner-up to American Tom Curren.

The following year, the worst period of his life, he fell back to twelfth place. At 23, to Barton's critics his world title run was over.

222

TONY NOLAN

People think of Barton as a calculating surfer, one who works as much on brain as brawn, as much on intellect as raw mindless talent. Maybe so, but he loves a surf as much as anyone.
Opposite: Trimming Pipeline.

"I'd never experienced such lows," Lynch recalled. "I'd lost the intensity needed for competition and was putting my energy into other areas. I started to question everything about myself – my surfing, my character – I went through a period of re-evaluation."

He decided to follow his own path again instead of looking up to the successful surfers. He knew he alternated between passion and lethargy and his surfing reflected this, so he worked on his intensity and concentration. He became stronger mentally and more aware.

The approach led him to being criticized for thinking too much. "That's utter crap," Lynch said. "Every successful surfer thinks, controls what's going on in their mind."

Ever the realist, Lynch knew he wasn't radical or innovative in the mold of Mark Occhilupo or Martin Potter, so he worked on making his surfing more spectacular. He aimed to loosen up his maneuvers and produce more vertical carves, with as much board out of the water as possible. In 1987 he climbed back to number three in the world. He was again a contender.

His greatest satisfaction in surfing is derived from trying to achieve excellence, basing his standards on competitive surfing.

"All the effort and time you've put into perfe-

cting your surfing is rewarded when you do well in competition. You know that all the training is not a waste of time, and you feel good about it."

Finally, in 1988, against all the odds (the only way Lynch knew how), he snatched the crown in the last contest of the year, the Billabong Pro at Banzai Pipeline, Hawaii.

He was even more satisfied that he had come from behind more favored opponents, Australians Tom Carroll and Damien Hardman, and triumphed in Hawaii, the greatest testing arena of all.

"Missing out so many times, then actually getting the thing in your hands – it was perfect. If I had written a script for myself I wouldn't have changed a thing," a relieved Lynch said after the victory.

But his critics didn't back off. People inferred that it was really Carroll's title, which had been lost on a technical interference in an earlier Billabong heat.

It was nothing new – Barton has always felt overlooked by the media, that he was never given the radical image or the push. He believes that it has cost him at critical times in his career when close judging decisions have gone to more favored surfers.

But as an honest, straightforward person he refuses to foster an image that isn't him: "I feel that I would be a lot more comfortable if the sport was more objective, as in who's first to cross the line or whatever. Then those image things wouldn't come into play as much . . . I just go about living my life as I am – as who I am – and let that go across as however it goes across."

There is no doubt that Lynch's adversities have spurred him on to great heights. In achieving his dream against all the obstacles, he has proved his tenacity as a fighter and his worth as a true surfing champion.

And he has also proved that it takes more than natural ability to be a great competitive surfer – an analytical, technical approach is also required in the new professional age.

As Barton put it: "Pure ability will only take you so far, then your head has to take you the rest of the way."

Martin Potter

TIM BAKER

The adjectives to describe Potter's surfing haven't yet been invented. "Radical" seems wimpy when pasted to his incredible aerial moves. **Opposite:** *A world champ at play.*

The label most often used to describe Martin Potter has been, the "world's most exciting free surfer." And for the first eight years of his career he seemed content with that title. His explosive surfing style wasn't suited to the competition demands for consistency and safety. And his temperament wasn't suited to the demands for dedication and discipline.

For eight seasons, since bursting on to the professional surfing scene at the tender age of 15, he maintained a Top 16 seeding almost purely on his freakish natural talent, and by his own admission, with "no effort whatsoever." In 1989, however, something clicked. He took out four of the first five contests in the most successful start to a season in the history of pro surfing. In comparison, the rest of his 89 season was characteristically patchy but he still could not be caught. At age 24, Martin Potter had defied the opinions of many seasoned pro surfing observers by taking out the world title.

Potter was born in northern England but he spent his formative years – from 2 to 15 – in South Africa. He didn't see the ocean until he was 10, started surfing at the relatively late age of 13, won the first contest he entered and was national junior champion at fourteen.

At 15, virtually unknown, he entered the two international pro contests that make up the South African leg of the world tour. In both contests he beat former world champion and South African national hero Shaun Tomson and finished second, in what remain pro surfing's most spectacular debut performances.

Inspired by his success in the South African events, he turned pro and joined the world circuit at 15, following the tour's chaotic path through Brazil, Japan, America, Hawaii and Australia. He finished the season eighth in the world. At just 16 years of age, and after only one season on the pro

tour, he had set the surfing world alight with his unique brand of power surfing and aerial maneuvers. It was an uncompromising approach that usually meant either spectacular success or spectacular failure in competition.

Many surfers have wrestled with the dilemma of translating spectacular free surfing into contest results; few have succeeded. That translation took nine years for Potter. While his 1989 world title campaign looked deceptively easy, it was, in fact, the climax of a tumultuous career. The rigors and constraints of competition almost became too much for Potter and he nearly turned his back on the contest trail more than once.

Gradually, though, Potter reconciled himself to the contest criteria. He has settled in Australia, on Sydney's northern beaches, found some much needed stability and a circle of friends, and a full-time manager in Peter Colbert, who had previously guided Tom Carroll to his two world titles. As Potter's powerful surfing became more controlled, his contest fortunes flourished. At the end of the 1989 season he'd taken the world title by the widest margin in pro surfing history and accumulated the biggest ever prize money total for a season – US$117,000.

Potter has also been credited with changing the public face of surfers. He wore his hair in long, unkempt dreadlocks, rarely shaved and openly acknowledges his taste for socializing, even during competition.

Potter's influence on the direction of surfing

DEAN WILMOT

has been profound. His world title came at a time when surfers were questioning the relevance of contest results as a valid measure of surfing talent. But even for the purists, there was no questioning the credentials of the world's most exciting free surfer as world champion. Potter is accomplished in almost all facets of the sport. He has proved his mettle in the big waves of Hawaii and his small-wave surfing is fast, powerful and dynamic. As he collected his 89 world title Potter commented, "I hope that if I do win it's going to be fashionable to just be able to go off and not worry – like, so what if you fall off a wave? You can go out and get another one."

Mark Richards

KIRK WILLCOX

There is no doubt that Mark Richards has been one of the most influential figures in the history of surfing.

Richards, from Newcastle, Australia, was there at the beginning of the world professional tour in 1976, when he finished third, and his record of four straight world titles from 1979 to 1982 is unlikely ever to be equalled.

But Richards was more than a world champion. He helped take a fledgling, shaky pastime of the 1970s and push it firmly into the new decade. In the 80s, surfing became recognized as a mainstream professional sport.

As one of the main spokespeople, Richards was intelligent, articulate and very down-to-earth; a normal human being who just happened to be a phenomenally gifted surfer.

There was no such thing as a career in professional surfing when he started competing in the early 1970s – Mark's ambition was to become a famous surfboard shaper. With his ungainly, knock-kneed style, which earned him the early

JEFF DIVINE

PAUL SARGEANT

*Amazingly enough, people used to laugh quietly behind Mark Richards's back about his surfing stance. They called him all sorts of cheeky nicknames, like "Wounded Gull," or worse, "Aeroplane." How foolish they looked later. **Spread**: MR laces Pipeline with an elegant spray. **Above**: Ready to hit Bells Beach, where he holds the record — four titles.*

nickname of "The Wounded Gull," that could well have been his fate.

But in 1977, looking for a competitive edge, Richards took the old twin-fin design and crafted it to his own specifications. In doing so, he took surfing from a down-the-line, tube-riding approach to one of fast, swooping maneuvers out on the face, punctuated by radical turns. Almost overnight, surfing's "wounded gull" had turned into a graceful bird.

The other professionals were forced to follow his lead. Fellow pro, Mike Tomson, remembers Mark pulling out a twin-fin at the first contest of 1978, the Stubbies Classic in Queensland.

While Richards didn't win the event, Tomson recalled that he would just go out and blitz – "whipping his board through maneuvers with such speed it left everyone slack-jawed in amazement. You had to be there to understand the impact, the fear and confusion which ripped through the pro ranks when MR connected on a wall at Burleigh. He was doing snaps off the top so fast it was scary." Typically, MR wasn't saying anything. Throughout his career he let his surfing speak for him. While the adulation flowed, he steadfastly remained himself. A fierce, calculating competitor whenever he pulled on the colored singlet, on land he was the exact opposite.

In fact, his biggest nerves came before a television interview, especially in his first year as world champion. He felt, rightly, that the public would judge the sport by him alone.

"If I went on TV and acted like an idiot or didn't speak coherently, the people sitting at home would go: 'See, I told you. They're just a bunch of drug addicts and dole bludgers,'" Richards recalled.

Within four years of his first title, the rejuvenated twin-fin led directly to Simon Anderson creating a counter in the three-fin thruster.

Both designs revolutionized the approach of the general surfing public around the world. But no one could surf a twinnie like MR – while he carved they generally flapped – and the design eventually fell to the advancement of the thruster.

Richards had come from behind to win his first championship unexpectedly, but from that point on he seriously defended it. After three titles he was satisfied with his achievements, but he was inspired to defend his crown once more when the media got behind Cheyne Horan in 1982.

"The media went berserk on Cheyne . . . that

gave me the push to pull it off again," Mark said.

After his fourth world title Richards competed only selectively, but in 1986 he recorded a career highlight by taking out the Billabong Pro at Waimea Bay in the most awesome surf of the decade.

On his way to victory he took off on the biggest wave he had ever caught in his life, a solid 25-footer (7.6 meters), and scored perfect 10s from the judges. He had also earned perfect 10s for a wave earlier in the day – for the first time in his long competitive career.

It was poetic justice. In the early days of pro surfing, the only way surfers were invited to contests was by establishing a reputation in Hawaii – taking off on the biggest, meanest waves.

"If we hadn't, you were just thought of as a wimp," Mark said. "And you'd never, ever, get a sponsor."

As fate would have it, his life turned full circle that day in 1986: "All my life all I've ever wanted was a big poster of myself surfing a giant wave at Waimea, a mountain. I'm a satisfied man now. I've got that photo."

So often in life, Richards, who is not the world's most confident person, pushed himself to prove he wasn't a wimp. He became a legend instead.

Once he was scared of big waves, like most surfers. Since then, he has won more Hawaiian events than any other competitor. Mark slices off the bottom at Sunset.

228

Nat Young

KIRK WILLCOX

With his huge feet, Robert "Nat" Young was destined to surf. But as he grew up in Australia in the 1950s, the sport was still in its infancy.

A decade later, with one world title under his belt, the single-minded rebel had influenced the approach of a whole nation and its future surfing champions. The name of the new game was power.

Nat started surfing on a monstrous longboard which he had to leave at the Collaroy Surf Club, on Sydney's northern beaches, because it was too heavy to carry home.

A tall, lanky kid, surfing totally consumed him, and he spent most of his time in the early 1960s between school and the beach, just like today's grommets.

The sport really captured the imagination of the Australian public when Bernard "Midget" Farrelly won the first World Championship at Manly Beach in 1964. As the leader of the Australian surfing fraternity, Midget had been one of Nat's heroes, in fact Nat had studiously copied his moves. Not long after the world titles, where Nat had reached the finals, he took out the Australian championship, defeating Farrelly.

While Nat had learnt traditional longboarding, which was based on long lines and a smooth flow with the wave, he took his natural aggression into the water and started attacking the wave at its power base – around the curl and in the pocket.

In retrospect, his early surfing days on cumbersome equipment had most likely led to enormous frustration in the impatient, spindly gremmie. "I could see how new things could be done on waves," he said later.

Working with shaper Bob McTavish and expatriate Californian designer George Greenough, 18-year-old Nat took a "short" board, a

229

Nat, the 1966 world surfing champ, was still holding the top spot in 1990 on the ASP longboard tour — a circuit he has done more to develop than anyone else.

9-foot 4-inch (2.8 meters) compared to the usual 10-footers, to the 1966 world titles in San Diego, California.

He had already earned the nickname "The Animal" for his radical approach and he reached the finals with heavies including Farrelly, Jock Sutherland and Corky Carroll. Californian favorite David Nuuhiwa had been knocked out earlier.

American Denny Aaberg remembers that Nat totally dominated the waves and the heat: "He

PETER CRAWFORD

was catching three waves to everybody's one. He rode on the edge, committed to the curl. His knife-railed board swung like an axe. It was a performance I'll never forget."

Virtually overnight, Nat's aggro approach changed the direction of world surfing. And the focus swung from hip California to upstart Australia. Within a year McTavish said the new Australian surfing was "around, on top of, and in the curl."

Nat admits he had a desperate competitive streak in his makeup and that competition inspired him. The late 60s became a frenzied period of surfboard experimentation, with boards becoming shorter and shorter and incorporating new design features like "V" bottoms and unorthodox fins, as surfers looked for a competitive edge.

"All this took so long to work through, taking all the good things," Nat said. "We would never have got all that power into turns, which became such an Australian trait, without Greenough's fins."

Nat was expected to win the world titles in Puerto Rico in 1968. Surfing journalist Drew Kampion recalls that he had grown stronger since 1966 and his boards had grown shorter.

"He exemplified the new surfing: deep, full-rail, carving turns; long tracks out onto the shoulder, then slam-bam back off the whitewater; rail-to-rail S-turns down the face leading into powerful, drawn-out bottom turns. He was the master; he'd have to break a leg to lose."

But Nat did lose, Farrelly was a standout and Hawaiian Fred Hemmings unexpectedly took the title.

After competing in the 1970 World Titles, Nat bailed out for about four years, competing only selectively in Hawaii.

He reappeared at the 1974 Surfabout in Sydney, picked up third place and publicly donated the money to Australian Labor Party prime minister, Gough Whitlam, on the steps of the Sydney Opera House. Nat was nothing if not dramatic.

He later ran for State parliament on Sydney's northern peninsula, campaigning heavily against beach pollution, and was only narrowly defeated.

Now in his forties, Nat is still a very active sportsman; he flies his own plane around the world, skis and surfs. He has also dabbled in modeling in the United States and produced a historical surfing film and books.

Nat came out of competitive retirement in the late 1980s to take out another couple of world titles in the professional longboard division, proving the fire has never died.

Nat has always refused to compromise, even today, and he admires a professional approach: "I don't care what it's in, if you're professional about everything you do. This has been my goal in life ever since I was a kid."

He still loves a wave. **Opposite**: *Nat drops down Trial Harbor in Tasmania.* **Below**: *Sometimes it's worth a chuckle even in a contest.*

PETER CRAWFORD

Frieda Zamba

MITCH VARNES

Once in a great while a person comes along who completely alters the state of an activity or changes the apparent course of history. Elvis Presley did it in the music industry, Mikhail Gorbachev has done it in the political arena and in the field of women's surfing, it has been Florida's Frieda Zamba.

The pre-Zamba era of women's wave riding was highlighted by long, graceful turns and a seemingly intentional avoidance of critical sections of the wave. While men were radically slashing mid-face cutbacks and snapping through-the-lip re-entries, women were elegantly carving along either the foot or shoulder of a wave. Competitors like Lynne Boyer, Margo Oberg, and Jericho Poppler were leading the charge and gradually pushing boundaries, but it wasn't until a sprightly 17-year-old Florida girl burst into the arena in 1982 and became the youngest female ever to win an ASP-rated event that women's surfing became the fiercely competitive and exciting spectator sport that it is today.

Wendy Botha, Pam Burridge, Jodie Cooper, Pauline Menczer and a handful of others have played big roles in women's surfing's newfound allure and have all established themselves as among the best, but it's Zamba who has largely been at the forefront of it all ever since winning

232

DOUG WATERS

her first ASP World Championship title in 1984. The 19-year-old goofyfoot took the circuit by storm that year when she managed to win five of the season's ten events and simultaneously become professional surfing's youngest world champion – a mark which still stands. Zamba's near-complete domination of women's surfing continued for the next two years as she became the first female ever to capture three straight world crowns. She relinquished the title to Wendy Botha in 1987 and took a leave of absence for most of that season to marry and homestead with her longtime coach and traveling companion, Flea Shaw. One year later Zamba was back on tour, back at the top and back at the ASP awards ceremony to acccept a record fourth world championship crown.

Zamba now surfs only selected contests but frequently still finds her way to the winner's circle in those she does enter. One of these recent victories came in the chilly waters of Santa Cruz, California, where the 25-year-old blasted past all competitors at the 1990 ASP season-opening O'Neill Coldwater Pro. Despite her ability regularly to beat longtime rivals and newcomers alike, Zamba has no intention of returning full-time to the demanding life of the world tour. Instead, she and Flea plan on spending the coming years building the business of Frieda's Surf Line, a surf shop they own and operate in the sleepy north Florida community of Flagler Beach.

International success has made Zamba the heroine of her home town and the most marketable female surfer in history. However, fame hasn't inflamed the ego of this slender and muscular surfer, who retains the laidback attitude and personality of her pre-glory days.

"I just happened to come along at a time when women's surfing needed a change; someone to stir the waters," she recalled. "For me, it's been unreal because I have always admired the great women surfers . . . and when I started surfing against them and actually beating them it was like a dream come true." Zamba credits the materialization of that dream to her choice of early surfing companions. "I grew up surfing around

*Frieda has been able to master any and all surfing conditions — one key reason why she stayed ahead of the pack for four world championships. **Opposite and below**: Wicked slashing at Typhoon Lagoon, Disney World, Florida.*

DOUG WATERS

some of the best guys on the East Coast, and that definitely made me surf more aggressively than I would have if I had just surfed with a girlfriend," she admitted.

Although she is not following the tour on a regular basis, Zamba still gets in the water every chance she gets. "I'm surfing for fun more than anything right now and trying to put a lot of energy into my business and personal life," she admitted. "That's not to say I'm letting up any competitively when I do enter contests. I'm just surfing in the events I want and going for the win in each. It gives me a lot of satisfaction to know I can still win contests and not have to worry about being world champion."

Her legacy to women's surfing can certainly be equated to an exciting new chapter of a book. "I guess you could say I led women's surfing beyond all the pretty fluff and put some radicalness into it," she reflected. "I think I'd like most to be remembered for leading a generation of women surfers."

GLOSSARY

aerial a maneuver where surfer and board become airborne

backside to surf with your back to the wave face. Another term is "backhand"

beach break surf where the waves are breaking onto a sand bottom directly off a beach

beavertail a form of wetsuit borrowed by surfers from skindivers in the 60s

berm area of coast just behind the first sand dune of a beach

blank raw foam or wood block from which surfboard shape is cut

bombora deepwater reef break where the broken wave fizzles out before breaking again nearer the shore

boomer big wave

bottom curve the curve through underside of surfboard from nose to tail

bottom turn turn which brings the surfer back up the face of the wave, often the first maneuver of a ride

bowl part or "section" of the wave where the wall bends back toward the oncoming foam

closeout a wave that breaks all at once along itself — no good for surfing!

cloud break deepwater reef break, similar to bombora

curl breaking part of a wave

cutback a maneuver in which the surfer banks the board through at least 90 degrees to drive back toward the curl

dumper wave that breaks violently, usually close to shore

face smooth unbroken area of wave beneath and ahead of the curl, where wave is steep enough for a surfer to gain speed and do maneuvers

first break old term for the point where the best waves begin to break offshore

floater a maneuver where the surfer slides the board across the top of the wave, often over foam or a crumbling lip, sometimes for several seconds before riding back down on to the face

flyer a surfboard design feature which involves a small bump or break in the rails, usually close to the tail. Originally known as a "wing"

frontside to surf facing the wave, opposite of "backside". Another term is "forehand"

full-rail turn a move, usually very difficult and spectacular, which involves the use of almost all a surfboard's length to drive a turn into the wave

goofyfooter surfer who rides with the right foot forward on the board

grommet young, very keen surfer. Also "gremmie"

gun surfboard used for riding big waves

hotdogging surfing with maximum number of turns and tricks allowed by the wave, usually in smaller surf

inside break where waves are reforming and breaking close to shore, after breaking properly further out

layback a maneuver where surfer half-falls off the board to swing it into a turn or ride inside the tube

legrope cord used to attach surfboard to a surfer's ankle, usually made from polyurethane. Also "leash"

lineup overall perspective of a surf spot, showing how the waves break

lip leading edge of a breaking wave; the part which comes down in front of the wave as it breaks

longboard surfboard designed after the fashion of the early 60s: usually over nine feet (2.7 meters), with wide rounded nose and single fin in tail. Also known as "logger" or "plank"

macker big wave; the derivation is "Mack truck"

Malibu board original sandwich-construction surfboard, made with a balsa core wrapped in resin and fiberglass. Now also refers to any longboard

naturalfoot surfer who rides with the left foot forward on the board

noseride a trick performed by standing on the nose of the board during a ride

ollie a skateboard trick where rider and board jump straight off flat ground into the air

olo a giant wooden surfboard, 16 to 18 feet (4.9 to 5.5 meters) long, used by ancient Hawaiian royalty

outside calm water beyond the breakers

paddleboard a board, usually longer and thicker than a standard surfboard, designed specifically for ocean paddling races

past vertical a situation where the bottom of a surfer's board is higher than the deck during a maneuver

pearl a wipeout where the nose of the board buries itself in the water, usually because the wave is too steep

pintail surfboard design where the tail ends in a point

pocket part of a breaking wave just beneath the curl

point break surf spot where waves run down the edge of a headland, over rocks or sand

rail the edges of a surfboard, where the top rolls over to meet the bottom

re-entry a maneuver in which surfer uses the breaking curl or lip of the wave to bring the board back down on to the face

rhino-chaser a big-wave surfboard; a play on "gun"

rocker curve through surfboard from nose to tail; also "bottom curve"

set group of waves, usually bigger than the ones immediately before or after

shaper a surfboard maker responsible for "shaping" the raw foam or wood blank into a rideable surfboard design

shore dump a wave which crashes directly onto a beach, possibly reforming after breaking further out. Not usually much good for surfing

shoulder unbroken part of wave ahead of the oncoming curl

sideslip a maneuver where the surfer's board slides sideways down the wave face (hopefully, with the surfer in control)

slam a skateboard term for "wipeout"

slot-fin a type of fin, used most often in sailboarding, where a small hole is cut to help control a board at speed

snapback a maneuver where a surfer performs a sudden direction change, usually back down the wave, while in the critical "pocket" area

soul surfing a non-competitive or anti-competitive surfing approach; i.e. surfing for "the good of your soul"

spinout, spinning out a situation where the surfboard's fins break free of the water during a turn, usually resulting in loss of control

stringer strip of wood running straight down the middle of a surfboard, usually for added strength

surf rats keen young surfers

swallowtail surfboard design in which the tail is split into two symmetrical points

swimfin flipper fitted to foot or feet for aid while swimming or bodyboarding

thruster surfboard design utilizing three fins of roughly equivalent size, one set on the stringer close to the tail with the others on either side. Invented by Australian shaper Simon Anderson in 1980

topturn a turn in the top half of the wave, usually to bring the board back down the wave face

trim a situation where the surfboard is set to run nicely at just the same speed as the wave

trim line the path across the wave on which trim can be achieved

tube ride part or all of a wave in which a surfer is enclosed by the curl, often being hidden if watched from the beach

twin-fin surfboard design utilizing two fins placed symmetrically on either side of the stringer close to the tail. Close relative of the thruster, popularized by Mark Richards

wipeout sometimes funny, sometimes horrible moment when a surfer falls off his or her board

zero break old term for the point at which the biggest swells of all break

WORLD CHAMPIONS THEN AND NOW

	MEN'S EVENT	WOMEN'S EVENT
1964*	Bernard "Midget" Farrelly (Australia)	Phyllis O'Donnell (Australia)**
1965*	Felipe Pomar (Peru)	No women's event
1966*	Robert "Nat" Young (Australia)	Joyce Hoffman (USA)**
1967*	No world championship	No world championship
1968*	Fred Hemmings (Hawaii)	Margo Godfrey (Hawaii)**
1969*	No world championship	No world championship
1970*	Rolf Aurness (USA)	Sharon Webber (Hawaii)**
1971*	No world championship	No world championship
1972*	Jim Blears (Hawaii)	Sharon Webber (Hawaii)**
1973–75	No world championships	No world championships
1976	Peter Townend (Australia)	Margo Oberg (Hawaii)**
1977	Shaun Tomson (South Africa)	Margo Oberg (Hawaii)
1978	Wayne "Rabbit" Bartholomew (Australia)	Lynne Boyer (Hawaii)
1979	Mark Richards (Australia)	Lynne Boyer (Hawaii)
1980	Mark Richards (Australia)	Margo Oberg (Hawaii)
1981	Mark Richards (Australia)	Margo Oberg (Hawaii)
1982	Mark Richards (Australia)	Debbie Beacham (USA)
1983	Tom Carroll (Australia)	Kim Mearig (USA)
1984	Tom Carroll (Australia)	Frieda Zamba (USA)
1985	Tom Curren (USA)	Frieda Zamba (USA)
1986	Tom Curren (USA)	Frieda Zamba (USA)
1987	Damien Hardman (Australia)	Wendy Botha (South Africa)
1988	Barton Lynch (Australia)	Frieda Zamba (USA)
1989	Martin Potter (UK)	Wendy Botha (Australia)

* These titles were all decided at big one-off shows called "world contests" and run as amateur events.
After 1972 the world contest machinery fell apart, to be replaced in 1976 by the world professional circuit.

** The women's world champion was not officially recognized until 1977 by the world tour;
Margo Oberg was declared unofficial champion in 1976.

CONTRIBUTORS

Tim Baker has surfed and traveled throughout the world. He was a journalist with the Melbourne *Sun–News–Pictorial* for two years and is currently editor of *Tracks* magazine in Sydney.

Wayne Rabbit Bartholomew was ranked in the top four of the ASP world tour for seven consecutive years; he was world champion in 1978. He retired from full-time pro surfing in 1987 and is now promotional director of Billabong Europe.

Nick Carroll is a hopeless surf addict who in the past has attempted to escape the tug of the ocean by working as a feature writer for the *Times on Sunday* (Sydney), the *Sydney Morning Herald*, *GH* magazine, *Village Voice* (New York) and the *Independent Monthly*. He is senior editor of *Surfing* magazine in California and lives too near the ocean for his own good.

Tom Carroll started surfing at Sydney's Newport Beach at the age of eight. He was twice world champion, and has held positions in the top five for the past eight consecutive years.

Rosaldo Cavalcanti was born in Brazil and grew up at Recife, Copacabana and Arpoador beaches. He is editor of *Now* surfing magazine and a contributing editor of *Surfer* magazine. He lives in Rio de Janeiro.

Richard Cram is a former Top 10 professional surfer and is currently managing director of Kadu Clothing.

Gary Dunne grew up in Sydney's beachside suburb of Curl Curl and began surfing at age 10. He is associate editor of *Tracks* magazine and was production editor of *Waves* magazine in 1989.

John Elliss is a former editor of *Tracks* magazine. Since 1988 he has been a freelance writer and is a surf reporter for radio station 2MMM in Sydney.

Terry Fitzgerald is a former Australian, Bells Beach and OM Bali champion. He is currently contest director for the Coca-Cola Classic and vice-president of the Australian Professional Surfers' Association (APSA).

Mark Foo is an award-winning sports journalist and surfer. He lives in Hawaii.

Matt George is a senior contributing editor to *Surfer* magazine in the United States.

Sam George is a senior editor of *Surfing* magazine in the United States, and has examined virtually every perspective of surfing, from stoked grommet to sponsored professional.

Paul Holmes started surfing in north Cornwall, England, at the age of 14. He has worked as a surfboard shaper and is a former editor of *Tracks* magazine. He was editor-in-chief of *Surfer* magazine in California, and is marketing director for Gotcha Clothing USA.

Derek Hynd is an Australia-based senior contributing editor to *Surfer* magazine. He was a member of the IPS world tour from 1979 to 1982 and has coached, among others, Mark Occhilupo, Jodie Cooper and Damien Hardman.

Rod Kirsop is a contributor to *Tracks* and *Waves* magazines. A big-wave addict, he has been an annual visitor to Hawaii for the past 11 years. He is senior registrar in obstetrics and gynecology at the Royal North Shore Hospital in Sydney.

Ryoji Kuribayashi is a contributing editor to *Surfin' Life* magazine in Japan and a former editor of *Surfing World*. He was born and raised in the Shonan area near Tokyo and has been surfing Shonan Beach for 15 years.

Michael Latronic is a professional surfer based in Hawaii and managing editor of *H30* magazine.

Leonard Lueras is a Bali-based editor-publisher-journalist who has either written, edited or produced some 20 books on Pacific area subjects. He was a reporter for the *Honolulu Advertiser* for more than 10 years.

Barton Lynch grew up surfing Whale Beach and Manly in Sydney, and began surfing professionally in 1981. He won the ASP world championship in 1988. He is managing director of Barlyn Pty Ltd and MD Control Shaping Pty Ltd.

Bill Sharp is the editor of California-based *Surfing* magazine and a contributor to surfing publications worldwide.

Mitch Varnes is a native of Florida who has surfed and written about most major East Coast surfing breaks from Nova Scotia, Canada, to Barbados. He is a freelance writer and East Coast editor of *Surfing* magazine.

John Veage has been a contributor to *Tracks* magazine since 1984 and is a newspaper photographer. A serious surfer and traveler for 15 years, he lives, and surfs, at Cronulla, Sydney.

Doug Warbrick surfed in the first world titles at Manly, Australia, in 1964. He founded Rip Curl Surfboards with Brian Singer in 1968, and was an ASP judge and contest official for a number of years.

Kirk Willcox is a former editor of *Tracks* and *Waves* magazines and a founding member of the environmental group Stop The Ocean Pollution (STOP). He writes a weekly surfing column for a major Sydney newspaper and surfs whenever he can find a clean day at Maroubra, his local beach on Sydney's southside.

Peter Wilson is an Australian freelance photo-journalist for surfing publications around the world, and until 1989 was advertising and promotions manager for surfwear manufacturer Quiksilver.

ACKNOWLEDGMENTS

The publishers would like to acknowledge the contribution of the following people in the production of this book: Leonard Lueras for help with archival material and illustrations; Larry Moore of *Surfing* magazine; Joanna Collard for assistance with picture research; Jack Eden, photographer; the Bishop Museum, Hawaii; all the photographers and archivists who submitted their work and collections for consideration; all the surfers who gave freely of their time to the writers and photographers; Doreen Grézoux for copy-editing the text, and Jan Smith for drawing the maps.

INDEX